The New Effective Voluntary Board of Directors

The New Effective Voluntary Board of Directors

What It Is and How It Works

William R. Conrad, Jr.

Swallow Press/Ohio University Press
ATHENS

Swallow Press/Ohio University Press, Athens, Ohio 45701
© 2003 by Swallow Press/Ohio University Press

Printed in the United States of America
All rights reserved

Swallow Press/Ohio University Press books are printed on acid-free paper ♾

11 10 09 08 07 06 05 04 03 5 4 3 2 1

Library of Congress Cataloging-in-Publication Data

Conrad, William R.
The new effective voluntary board of directors : what it is and how it
works / William R. Conrad, Jr.
   p. cm.
   Rev. ed. of: The effective voluntary board of directors. c1983.
   Includes bibliographical references.
   ISBN 0-8040-1033-1 (alk. paper) — ISBN 0-8040-1034-X (pbk. : alk.
paper)
   1. Associations, institutions, etc.—Management. 2. Directors of
corporations. 3. Voluntarism. 4. Boards of directors. I. Conrad, William R.
Effective voluntary board of directors. II. Title.

HV41.C644 2003
658.4'22—dc21

                                                    2003042714

Contents

Section IV: How to Assemble a Board

Section V: How a Board Operates

Section VI: What Can Go Wrong and How to Fix It

Illustrations

Acknowledgments

First and foremost, thanks to my wife Helen for her unreserved support. I owe everything to her. When I first started out on my own she gave me a button that said "Follow Your Dream." It is beside my desk always and remains my inspiration.

As in the previous two editions, I want to recognize my fallen friend and colleague, James C. Manning. Our friendship was all too short, but his spirit has always been with me.

I am working with an outstanding group of professionals who have offered wisdom and support. I wish to acknowledge them here. They form our Board of Contributors and I thank them:

Del Arsenault, President and CEO (ret.), Chicago Youth Centers

Karl H. Benne, Senior Consultant, Health Canada-Voluntary Health Sector, Ottawa, Ontario, Canada

Greg Darnieder, Executive Director, Steans Family Foundation

Karen Girolami Callam, Independent Consultant

Rev. Stanley Davis, Executive Director, NCCJ, Chicago and Northern Illinois Region

Ed Guerrero, Director of Human Resources, Catholic Charities

Susan Halbert, Senior Vice President, Organizational Systems & Development, National 4-H Council, Chevy Chase, MD

Margaret Harris, Ph.D., Professor of Voluntary Sector Organisation, Aston Business School (PSM group), Aston University, Birmingham, England xii Acknowledgments

Mary Ann Mahon-Huels, Executive Director, Union League Boys & Girls Clubs

April Janney, Assistant Vice President for Operations, Boys & Girls Clubs of Chicago

George Jones, Executive Director, Ada S. McKinley Community Services

Janet M. Knupp, President, The Chicago Public Education Fund

Virginia Ladd, President and CEO, American Autoimmune Association, Detroit, MI

Tim Mills-Groninger, Associate Executive Director, IT Resource Center

BG Ronald Scott Mangum, Commanding General, Special Operations Command, Korea

Denis Murstein, Administrator, Youth Network Council

Sylvia Puente, Project Director, Institute for Latino Studies, University of Notre Dame

Ted O'Keefe, Director, 311 City Services, City of Chicago

Faith Smith, President, NAES College (Native American Educational Services)

Carlos Tortolero, Executive Director, Mexican Fine Arts Center Museum

Over the years, I have worked with many board members and board chairpersons who have enhanced my knowledge and skills significantly. It seems appropriate for me to acknowledge those who stand out for their contributions to voluntary action and to my personal and professional growth. Without them, this book would not have been written. They are special people.

Mrs. Lester Crown, Chicago, IL

Calvin Fentress, Jr., former Chairman, Allstate Insurance Company, Chicago, IL

Louis E. Martin, former editor, *Chicago Defender* and special advisor to President Carter, Chicago, IL

Emory M. Nelson, National Council of the YMCA, Chicago, IL

James J. O'Connor, former Chairman, Commonwealth Edison, Chicago, IL

Walter H. Sanderson, former President, Sanderson Industries, Orlando, FL

W. Clement Stone, former Chairman, Combined Insurance Company, Chicago, IL

Ozell E. Greene, Greene's Groceries, Chicago, IL

Miriam Torrado, Chicago, IL

Finally, I wish to thank those who put my scribblings into a book. Geri-Ann Marzullo Ortega did much of the computer work and coordinated the efforts that resulted in this book. Liz Vacariello, a longtime friend and colleague, spent many evenings at the computer. And my sister-in-law, Nancy Semenek, took a week off to work at the computer.

Introduction

Before entering into a prolonged examination of how the boards of voluntary organizations operate, we should first agree upon certain assumptions. Before all, we must agree that boards make a difference. Although this seems to go without saying, there are some who feel that boards no longer matter, that professionals can run their organizations very well without the interference of boards.

Led with confidence and inspiration within a clear and workable framework, *boards make a difference*. I have seen too many excellent boards to feel any other way. When a board *does not* make a difference, it is because neither its members nor the staff is committed to making the board effective. In today's complex society, boards are more important than ever. Staff must have cooperation, assistance, and information sharing from their board if they are to be successful and if their organization is to serve the community effectively.

Some feel that the current board models are no longer feasible, that a new governance model is about to be discovered. One wonders what we are to do in the interim. Is it the proper role of voluntary organizations to act as laboratories for management theory? There are fundamental concepts and principles that will, if followed, result in an effective board. Let's not create new models. Let's make the old ones work.

Do boards make sense for every sort of organization? Perhaps there is something to be gained by experimenting in the way I warn against above. After all, I have never met a board that did not insist that it was unique. I have never encountered a board that did not insist that it faced challenges faced by no other organization. There are, in fact, threads of consistency that run through *all* voluntary boards. All boards develop conceptually and methodologically according to the challenges they face, but they do so as *boards,* not as some other managerial structure.

Often, in attempting to answer common organizational anxieties, the cry goes up: "Nonprofits must become more businesslike." Rather than seeking to adapt business models to work in a nonprofit environment, this cry signals an attempt to overhaul the entire culture. Since no one, in my experience, is quite sure what makes a nonprofit a nonprofit, adaptation simply becomes *adoption,* an easier but more harmful step.

Later in this book, I argue that although there is no question that nonprofits can be better led and managed, we first need to understand what better nonprofit leadership and management means. Leadership and leadership concepts are not the sole property of business. The real challenge before us is to make nonprofits more "nonprofitlike." As Brian O'Connell, President of the Independent Sector, once remarked before the Professional Education Forum: "Everything tracks back to our need to have a clearer understanding of the unique functions of government, business, and nonprofit organizations and the importance of not judging any one of the three according to standards that do not give principal emphasis to their unique role."

We must use the best of our two sister sectors, business and public: Adopt what fits, adapt what we can, and create what we need.

Legal realities must be considered as well. Governance, in the legal sense, cannot exist in a nonprofit organization without a board. Whether the board governs effectively is, of course, another question. But governance does not exist without boards.

Boards can rise to any challenge so long as members remain loyal to the organization and to the purpose for which the organization was formed. It is only the weak board members who will fade away at the first inkling of trouble or controversy. There is no question that the time available for individuals to serve on boards has diminished. Corporate mergers, downsizing, increased commitment to family, longer work hours, and so on, have caused a scarcity of discretionary time. However, there are still ample prospective board members to be found. Staff members do believe in boards and view their boards as partners. Yes, there are horror stories; but most staff still believe in the concept of boards. As long as voluntarism and democracy thrive, the conditions for effective boards will exist.

Effective boards do not just happen. If we think of an art as exceptional skill in conducting any human activity and a science as a way of thinking whose goal is to discover the workings of the world based on experiment, then working with boards is an art as well as a science. It is an art in that the most difficult job in the world is working with people. The art of good board work *is* "conducting human activity," molding a diverse group into an effective whole for the good of an organization. It is also a science in that one must also be knowledgeable about *what* must be done to make the parts a whole. Again, this requires concepts, procedures, roles, and functions that are known, understood, and agreed upon. The successful board member, like the successful staff member, is neither an artist nor a scientist; he or she is a delicate blend.

We in the voluntary field simply cannot serve people on faith alone; we need systems, structures, dollars, and above all, *people.* Without these, faith flounders and is replaced by despair and disillusionment. Any outward thrust in terms of service must be matched by effective, self-renewing systems and structures.

1

Point of View

Over my many years of teaching, leading workshops, and speaking, one of my most difficult tasks has been to understand the audience's point of view. I'm not alone in this. "What concerns me," remarked the philosopher Epictetus, "is not the way things are, but rather the way people think things are." We needn't go back as far as Epictetus, however, to find examples of this age-old problem. "We lack even the elementary grasp of the fundamental idea that one communicates within the experience of his audience," writes Saul Alinsky in *Rules For Radicals*, "[giving] full respect to the other's values." Because all humans have had differing experiences in life, no two individuals will hold exactly the same point of view. The key to understanding human behavior is to recognize that every event or situation is interpreted differently by each person who witnesses it.

We might also say that beliefs and point of view are derived from a *frame of reference*, or a structure of concepts, principles, values, and customs against which an individual assigns meaning to data that regulate his or her behavior. It follows that if we wish to influence beliefs and point of view of an individual, we must establish a clear frame of reference, either by creating a new one or else by modifying or even expunging an existing one. One of our greatest problems in board leadership is that of shifting frames of reference.

For example, a new staff executive or board chair might change the existing board's frame of reference by implementing a so-called "business model" of management without allowing adequate time for discussion and adjustment among staff and other members of the organization. A too-rapid shifting of an established frame of reference is often at the heart of board dysfunction. Each time a frame of reference shifts, an individual's belief system and point of view can become confused, causing what we'll call *cognitive dissonance*.

Cognitive dissonance is a major cause of miscommunication, but often goes unrecognized. Discourse consonant (consistent) with a person's beliefs causes that person to feel pleased, relaxed, and calm. But should the discourse prove dissonant (inconsistent) with those beliefs, the same person will try to reduce the dissonance, perhaps by denying the speech or discussion ever occurred or by developing a web of rebuttals. A final response to dissonance, unhappily familiar to us all, is to ridicule or derogate the source of the dissonant information. Whatever the response, any idea following the moment of dissonance is lost because the individual is busy concentrating on the rationale for his or her contrary beliefs. Individuals will do almost anything before giving up prior beliefs or mental habits.

Dissembling is a close relative of cognitive dissonance. Those who dissemble conceal their feelings and motives. They put up pretenses because it is uncomfortable or dangerous to do otherwise. Dissembling undermines honest discussion and silences conflicting opinions. We must keep an open mind, even while adhering to a basic set of principles. In a sector of the economy that outwardly supports new thinking, it won't do for nonprofit leadership and management to remain rigid and arrogant on this score.

Over the years I have listened to board members and staff talk past each other. Sometimes they engaged in stereotyping, exaggerating or oversimplifying each other's views. At other times they spoke and responded only according to habit, forgoing the possibility of new ideas and change. There was often much conversation, but little communication. Everyone was speaking English, but the words themselves carried little generally understood and accepted meaning. One day it occurred to me that the phenomenon I was observing was based on cultural differences.

Culture consists of values, beliefs, knowledge, art, customs, and habits that lie behind the behavior of people. Culture also establishes standards shared by members of a society or organization which, when acted upon, produce behavior that falls within what is considered the acceptable range.

How a culture perceives itself is reflected in its language. Therefore language will influence, if not determine, what an individual will notice in his or her environment.

Board members often move between several board cultures. If a particular culture becomes uncomfortable, they fall into what is known as *culture shock*. The reaction to culture shock varies according to the individual, of course. Sometimes they simply withdraw. Other members try to take over and show everyone how "it ought to be done." The most sophisticated board members adapt. They understand that all cultures are unique and are best evaluated according to internal standards and values.

The first response to culture shock, that of the member who continues to show up for meetings but has less and less to say, can be almost as damaging as that of the self-elected leader who simply discards those aspects of board culture he or she finds encumbering. Neither member is contributing to—or relying upon—the strengths inherent to boards. In either case, the crisis manifests itself in the language used by participants in the discussion. As E. D. Hirsch, Jr., wrote in *Cultural Literacy*, "[A] human group must have effective communications to function effectively, . . . effective communications require shared culture, and . . . shared culture requires transmission of specific information."

We must be especially careful in our use of language when working on nonprofit boards. Words convey ideas. Ideas provide the basis for points of view. Therefore, the language we use to convey those ideas carries with it a distinct point of view and may influence the behavior of the listener. There is no hope for effective communication unless we can agree upon the meanings of words based on shared cultural norms. As Confucius said, "If language be not in accordance with the truth of things, affairs cannot be carried on to success."

Let's consider a few amusing examples of the tension between point of view and language. Perhaps you remember the following old poem:

> Six wise men of India
> An elephant did find
> And carefully they felt its shape
> (For all of them were blind).
>
> The first he felt towards the tusk,
> "It does to me appear,

This marvel of an elephant
Is very like a spear."

The second sensed the creature's side
Extended flat and tall,
"Ahah!" he cried and did conclude,
"This animal's a wall."

The third had reached towards a leg
And said, "It's clear to me
What we should all have instead
This creature's like a tree."

The fourth had come upon the trunk
Which he did seize and shake,
Quoth he, "This so-called elephant
Is really just a snake."

The fifth had felt the creature's ear
And fingers o'er it ran,
"I have the answer, never fear,
The creature's like a fan!"

The sixth had come upon the tail
As blindly he did grope,
"Let my conviction now prevail
This creature's like a rope."

And so these men of missing sight
Each argued loud and long
Though each was partly in the right
They all were in the wrong.

This is my adaptation of the venerable "Blind Men and the Elephant":

There were seven honest citizens
Who joined a board with much to do,
And eagerly they went to work,
Each with a point of view.

The first was a CPA who said,
"It's obvious for all to see
The major problem to be solved,
Is one of accountancy."

The second was a business type,
Who forcefully did say,
"Let my conviction now prevail,
We must adopt the business way."

The third was a grocery owner,
Who firmly did entreat,
"We must make our neighborhood safe again,
By taking kids off the street."

The fourth was a lawyer of high repute,
"It does appear to me,
The issue we must first address,
Is legal liability."

The fifth was a marketing exec,
Who had to speak before she burst,
"No, no, my friends! It's very clear.
A marketing plan is first."

The sixth was a resident,
A community view did bring,
"I have the answer, never fear,
Our program is the thing."

The seventh, a respected member of many boards,
Said, "Our success is guaranteed,
By virtue of my experience,
If you'll follow my lead."

And so these honest citizens,
Each argued loud and long,
Though each was partly in the right,
They all were in the wrong.

I think visual examples never hurt. Figure 1-1 shows two cartoons that beautifully demonstrate the point-of-view problem.

Point of View in Practice

Having learned from these experiences, I now start my workshops and classes with a discussion of point of view. I ask participants to list the missions or purposes of their respective organizations, to set forth the beliefs or values of their organizations, to define board policy (the decisions their boards actually make), and to outline the most important policy decision their board makes. I refer to these four questions as the *Four Fundamental Areas of Agreement*. An organization must have universal understanding and agreement on these four points. Without this understanding and agreement, there can be no rational and effective decision-making process.

Over the years there has been a remarkable consistency across very

Figure 1–1. The problem of point of view. Reprinted with the gracious permission of Bonnie Hoest and John Reiner

disparate groups. About half of the group can define their board's mission and purpose (or at least come close), while only about a quarter of the group knows whether the beliefs or values statement even exists. Often, there are nearly as many definitions of policy as there are participants. About ninety percent of the group identifies hiring the staff chief executive as its most important policy decision. (Do you agree? Make a note. The question will be answered later in the book.)

In Chicago, I use another technique that is both fun and instructive. I pass out a street map and ask participants to draw a circle around one of the world's greatest intersections, State and Madison. Some find it quickly, while others sit baffled. Usually, I have to point out that the map I've passed out is of Milwaukee. Lake Michigan is to the east of both Chicago and Milwaukee, and the street configuration is very similar. There is a State and Madison, after all, but the streets seem to run the wrong direction to someone from Chicago. Unless the board and staff are following the same map, neither will get anywhere. No meaningful dialogue can take place without a common frame of reference and point of view. Without this, all we have is a series of monologues.

The balance of this book is devoted to establishing a clear, balanced, and useful basis to construct a frame of reference for conducting a board's business.

2

The Work of a Nonprofit

Diversity of all sorts is the source of the nonprofit sector's great strength and of its many contributions to civil society. In the leadership and management issues facing nonprofits today, however, diversity can actually become a block to an organization's effectiveness. Consider the diversity among the types of nonprofits. They range from the completely volunteer-led, small community organizations, to huge national and multinational organizations such as hospitals and universities. They cover an almost limitless spectrum of missions, sizes, and complexities. Board members who serve on a number of different boards of directors find differing cultures and methods of operation in each organization. Managing these differences, this diversity, can lead to confusion and inertia.

Over my many years in the nonprofit field, I've noticed certain constants across all nonprofit organizations, regardless of mission, size, or complexity. These constants can be modeled in four dimensions: people, framework, leadership/management, and community. This chapter, however, will discuss only the framework dimension.

While I was teaching one of my early graduate classes at George Williams College, we began to discuss all the tasks a nonprofit organization had to accomplish. We developed the following list:

program	hiring/firing	office management
buildings	personnel	fund raising
insurance	board	board development
budget	staff	publicity
public relations	volunteers	recognition
purchasing	salary	accounting
training	performance evaluation	risk management
computer	community outreach	financial statements

Later that week, I happened to watch an episode of the PBS series *NOVA*, titled "The Shape of Things." The show explored the thesis that there are six basic shapes—sphere, polygon, spiral, helix, meander, and branch—that appear in nature over and over again. These basic shapes, as the argument went, in different and more or less complex combinations, are the building blocks making up the natural world. I was intrigued enough to order a transcript. The program ended with these wonderful paragraphs:

> Throughout nature, basic shapes are shared by natural objects and organisms as diverse as feathers and trees, snails and sunflowers, honeycombs and snowflakes.
> Form comes from growth or from the way forces affect materials. Shapes are influenced by factors ranging in scale from the molecular to the environmental. The wind, the weather, and even the force of gravity are a few of the conditions imposed on shapes of all sizes.
> But these constraints are not necessarily limitations; they are opportunities for new variations on old themes. Their beauty is the outward appearance of orderly structure.
> Basic shapes are only the beginning of the story. They lead to an understanding of structure in all living things because they are often the building blocks of more complex organisms. The need to conserve energy creates order. Disarray is wasteful of the materials and energy with which life confronts the environment.
> It is not always apparent why things are shaped the way they are, but nature is constantly creating similar forms over and over again. Within the diversity of nature there is order, and as the home of life, earth is the planet of shapes.

Watching this show and thinking about the idea of an infinite variety of complex structures arising from a small number of basic shapes, I began to see a parallel with the discussions in my class earlier in the week. Perhaps it wasn't too much of a stretch to say that the wide variety of forms evident among nonprofit organizations derived from a relatively small number of basic elements common to all of them. Perhaps we could apply the "shapes" concept to the nonprofit sector. It struck me that the tasks the class and I had been discussing actually constituted the *work* of nonprofits. Keeping in mind nature's shapes, I took another look at the list of tasks the class had drawn up. We had written the list on newsprint sheets, allowing me to cut out each individual task and tape it to the wall.

I moved the slips of paper around to form what seemed to be natural groups. Once all the slips had been grouped, I could see how they formed the basic "shapes" that make up a nonprofit. Although the names of the tasks or their groupings may vary from one nonprofit organization to the next, the work still has to be done in every organization. The following categories emerged:

1. Purpose/Mission/Values/Beliefs
2. Vision
3. Leadership/Management
4. Technology
5. Service Delivery
   (1) Program Services
6. Support to Service Delivery
   (1) Resource Development
   (2) Finance
   (3) Human Resources

The following is the original list from my class. Opposite each entry is its position in the new arrangement—what I call the *Work to Be Done*.

Program	Program Services
Buildings	Property
Insurance	Property
Budget	Finance
Public relations	Resource Development
Purchasing	Finance
Training	Human Resources
Hiring/firing	Human Resources
Personnel	Human Resources

Board	Leadership/Management, Resource Development
Staff	Leadership/Management, Human Resources
Volunteers	Resource Development
Salary	Human Resources
Performance evaluation	Human Resources
Office management	Finance
Board development	Leadership/Management, Resource Development
Publicity	Resource Development
Recognition	Resource Development, Human Resources
Accounting	Finance
Computer	Technology
Community outreach	Image, Program
Financial statements	Finance

Figure 2–1 shows my basic model of the work of a nonprofit organization, a structure into which specific tasks may be plugged.

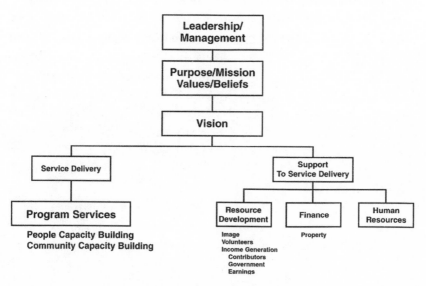

Figure 2–1. The Work to Be Done

A more detailed breakdown of the "Support to Service Delivery" category would look like this:

I. Resource Development
   (1) Image
   (2) Public relations and publicity
   (3) Volunteers
       (i) Board, advisors, staff
   (4) Income generation
       (i) Contributions, government, earned
II. Finance
   (1) Finance
       (i) Budgeting, accounting, purchasing, payroll, investment management, legal, inventory, audit, financial statements, insurance
   (2) Property
       (i) Land, buildings, equipment, office management, maintenance, risk management
III. Human Resources
   Including: Legal, hiring, orientation, rules and working conditions, compensation, unions, transfers, promotion, staff development, employee benefits, rotation, employee and community relations, separation, performance appraisal

Some consider a functional arrangement like this one to have inherent dangers. Chief among these is overspecialization, meaning that the staff members working within a particular function become expert at that function, but have little knowledge or interest in the total work of their organization. This can splinter an organization into competing components. It is important that every member of an organization, whether volunteer or salaried staff, understands the scope of the organization's work. This broad-based understanding will help the organization to avoid the trap of overspecialization.

To illustrate this issue, I introduce my groups to the *Hoberman Sphere*. The Hoberman Sphere is an unfolding structure made of slightly curved links joined into "scissor-pairs." These pivots allow the sphere to contract and expand. My sphere is about eight inches in diameter when contracted and expands to thirty-four inches when fully opened. My point is that although the Work to Be Done chart is a linear model, operationally an organization should function like the sphere: always connected, no matter how large it becomes. Each participant receives a miniature Hoberman Sphere.

Every nonprofit organization must somehow manage all (or most) of the work identified here. Different organizations may use different terms to describe this work: universities may call program services "curriculum" and resource development "external affairs"; a hospital may call program services "patient care." Some nonprofits may not have work in all of the categories—a group might have no buildings or land, but might have equipment; another might not utilize staff volunteers. Organizations may delegate and oversee the work differently: larger organizations might have one staff person responsible for each category, small ones only one staff person or volunteer responsible for the entire spectrum of work.

All nonprofit organizations must develop their own Work to Be Done models. It is the basis for strategic planning and many other aspects of non-profit leadership and management, including policy definition, identification and work of committees, and criteria for board members.

3

The Delicate Balance
Harmony, but Not at Any Price

Letting the inevitable differences that arise within an organization go unresolved invites factionalism. The day when everyone has to choose sides is the day when organizational goals and devotion to the organization's ideals are lost. There is tension in any relationship between two or more people or two or more groups. Whether this tension produces growth or is simply destructive depends upon how well the relationship maintains its balance, or *homeostasis*.

Think of how a violin string requires tension to sing. Too much tension, and the string breaks; too little tension, and the string goes slack.

Balance is never absolute. It can tip slightly one way or another, but always seeks a natural equilibrium. If a nonprofit organization cannot maintain this equilibrium, the nonprofit organization will ultimately be destroyed. Let's refer to this equilibrium as the *delicate balance*.

There is a dynamic tension between the two ends of the bar shown in Figure 3-1. However well the two ends work together, a tension will always exist between them. This is natural, as they are interdependent. It has been my observation that this dynamic tension fosters creativity. For example, when I

Figure 3-1. The Delicate Balance—1

worked with Calvin Fentress, Jr., former chairman of the board of Allstate Insurance, his demands for solutions to the problems we encountered in fundraising for the Boys and Girls Clubs of Chicago *always* stimulated my creative juices. Later, after I left the Boys and Girls Clubs, he said that he had appreciated the "diplomatic demands" I had made and that they had caused him to rethink long-held beliefs. It is unlikely that we would have enjoyed such success in fundraising if there hadn't been that tension between us.

Without tension, nothing much can happen—save stagnation and deterioration. An excess of tension, however, results in conflict, frustration, and collapse. Notice that the bar balances on a fulcrum. This fulcrum has a critical effect on the maintenance of the delicate balance, as we will see in a moment.

The two large, outer circles are also important. The first symbolizes the organization which contains the delicate balance. The outside circle symbolizes the community within which the organization exists and with which the organization must maintain a balance.

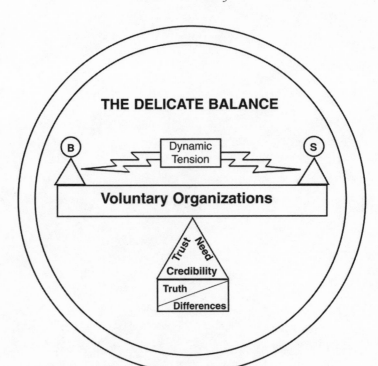

Figure 3-2. The Delicate Balance—2

Let's see how the delicate balance really operates in a nonprofit organization. First, we will explore the delicate balance between the board and staff. Figure 3-2 illustrates the importance of the fulcrum on which the delicate balance of dynamic tension rests. This fulcrum comprises three elements: *need, credibility,* and *trust.* Need is based, above all, on the understanding and acceptance of the respective roles played by the board and staff. Board members and staff need each other if they are to succeed in assuring the effectiveness of their organization.

As the board and staff work effectively within their respective roles, each gains credibility in the eyes of the other. Confidence emerges. Once board and staff establish this mutual credibility and confidence, trust develops. Trust does not mean the absence of difference—it means that no matter the difference, the board and staff can find reasonable ground to mediate that difference. People who trust each other have neither the need nor the desire to develop hidden agendas.

Trust takes on four dimensions in the human service nonprofit organization:

Reliability: We tend to trust people who do what they say they will do.

Acceptance: Trusting people accept each other and rarely become judgmental.

Openness: Trust is built on openness—by saying what one thinks. As a board chairperson once said, "I'll accept a lot because things do happen. But do not surprise me!"

Purpose: An absolute commitment to organizational purpose and values/beliefs without deviation. Let purpose be the directional compass of a program; let values/beliefs be the ethical compass or ethos.

Each of these dimensions depends upon truthfulness. Truth is often inconvenient. Truth is often uncomfortable. Too often the truth is ignored or modified for the sake of some convenience, such as "not rocking the boat" or "not upsetting the boss." Facts that are not honestly faced have a habit of stabbing us in the back. As Will Schutz once wrote, "Trust is the great simplifier. If people in business organizations told the truth, 80 to 90 percent of their problems would disappear. That's the biggest lesson corporate America could learn." Truth is often sacrificed at the altar of avoiding accountability. Yet without truth need, credibility, and trust cannot survive—let alone thrive.

Some leaders do not want the truth. They stifle dissent. They do not wish to hear from those who may have a different point of view or who may simply be right. These leaders are sunk in the sea of their own arrogance and ignorance. We might say that they have lost their ethical compass.

The lack of tolerance for truth, at least as others see truth, has another critical consequence. Unless a leader hears and understands the "truth" of others, the leader will never have the full range of options necessary to make viable decisions. That is to say, no one person can ever have all the information or control all the variables required to make decisions. A leader who cuts himself or herself off from the opinions of others will never have all the data needed to make a wise and informed decision.

Strong leaders characteristically have a strong vision, but good leaders have a sufficient sense of personal security to tolerate input that keeps this vision from drifting into fantasy. Insecure leaders have no tolerance for such input. Over time, they surround themselves with "yes persons" who, in the interests of their own gain, offer constant reinforcement of the leader's fantasies. Those who attempt to communicate reality, at least as they see it, are pushed aside or worse. Contrary to popular opinion, most people can deal with the truth.

Need, credibility, and trust require the recognition and acceptance of differences, just as they require respect for the truth. At the heart of any difference are three critical and interrelated principles: the necessity of cooperation, the inevitability of differences, and the avoidance of conflict. For example, my relationship with Cal Fentress was a sound one because we trusted each other and because we were secure in the knowledge that our opinions were grounded in what was best for the young people who were members of the Boys and Girls Clubs. Each of us understood that the delivery of services to those young people depended upon an acceptance of the other's role.

We had to *cooperate.*

To cooperate, we *acknowledged* the inevitability of differences.

We *resolved* our differences before they escalated into polarization and conflict.

Encourage difference, for it is from difference that we grow. Innovation and progress come from differences. Nothing is ever achieved when everyone thinks and behaves in the same way. The challenge difference puts before us is that of finding rational grounds for mediation before the difference can escalate to conflict. Trust is, of course, the basis for rational mediation. When you trust someone, you believe in that person's integrity, character, and ability. Though you may differ, you trust him or her and can maintain a productive and healthy interaction. Board members must denounce any intolerance of difference, for such intolerance inevitably leads to some form of persecution.

Often the scars of conflict are deep and destroy long-term cooperation. I am reminded of a certain arts organization, which had a budget of more than $2,000,000 per year. A conflict developed between the executive director and the musical director concerning their respective roles. A year passed before the board even became aware of this increasingly hostile relationship. The board, through its chair, moved to reduce the conflict and to establish a *modus vivendi* between the two disputants, but it was already too late. What began as a rational approach to solving the conflict soon failed. The board factionalized around the two individuals, and the dispute was carried into the public realm.

To keep differences from escalating into conflict, members must remember, above all, that differing viewpoints are not wrong, inferior, or strange. They must know the difference between what is essential and what is merely important. They must also guard against premature judgments, maintain open minds, and interact based on that increased awareness. Heed Seneca's warning: "Everyone prefers belief to an exercise in judgment." There is a certain security in holding on to long-standing beliefs, even when those beliefs are no longer useful or valid. All incoming information is measured against these beliefs, eliminating the need to judge or evaluate the new information on its own merits.

Members must also remember the inherent strength of board organization: that some of the best ideas come from others, that the group is stronger than the individual. Any negotiations, accommodations, or compromises must be made without violating the organization's basic principles, concepts, and values.

The arts organization in our earlier example did not take these precepts to heart. Because the conflict between the board and the two staff members was not resolved, staff resigned and the community—disenchanted with the very public squabbling—withdrew its support both financially and through decreased attendance at organization events. The organization closed.

There are many balances to be found within any nonprofit, all of them subject to the same principles as the board-staff relationship discussed above. The board chairperson and members have interests that must be balanced delicately. Sometimes there is an internal board added to the mix. The organization as a whole must, of course, strike a balance with the community it serves. Other important balances within the nonprofit organization include:

Board chairperson and staff
Committee chairperson and committee members
Committee chairperson and staff liaison
Internal staff
Volunteer and staff

It isn't hard to think of other dynamic pairings—in fact, you can be sure

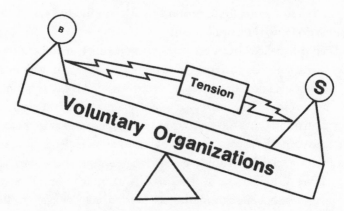

Figure 3-3. The Delicate Balance—3

that any position depicted on the organization chart or value espoused in the charter has its counterpart which must be brought into balance.

Sadly, these delicate balances are disturbed all too often. Earlier, I suggested that nature seeks equilibrium. So it is with the nonprofit organization. Should one side weaken, the other gains strength in proportion.

In Figure 3-3, board members are reduced to yea-sayers. Generally, when confronted with this situation, the *truly* good board volunteers depart rather quickly! Voluntarism is in trouble today partly because this very situation applies to so many of our nonprofit organizations. It is interesting to note that many of the financial troubles of nonprofit organizations are not really financial problems, but rather board problems. Simply put, uninvolved

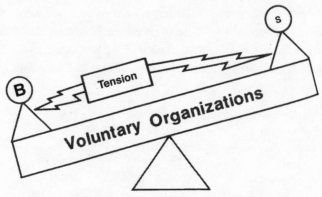

Figure 3-4. The Delicate Balance—4

board volunteers will not fund an organization. Many organizations in financial trouble are out of balance because of over-professionalism. Trust, credibility, and need vanish. Dynamic tension becomes mere tension.

In Figure 3-4, the organization has become overly board-oriented without staff involvement. As in the previous chart, trust, credibility, and need vanish, and dynamic tension again becomes tension.

Purpose and vision are achieved only through cooperation. Purpose and vision may begin with the work of one member or a few, but must come to be shared by the whole organization, working cooperatively to bring this vision to reality. Chester I. Barnard in his classic 1938 book, *The Functions of the Executive,* wrote: "The initial concept of cooperation leads to the definition of organization as a 'system of consciously coordinated activities or forces of two or more persons.' Essential to the survival of organization is the willingness to cooperate, the ability to communicate, the existence and acceptance of purpose."

Section 1

What a Board Is For

4

Boards: What Do They Do?

Boards exist, first and foremost, because state and federal law mandate that every nonprofit shall have one. Everyone involved with nonprofits, whether volunteer or staff, agrees on this fundamental point. After that, as I pointed out in chapter 1, there are many points of view about the functions of nonprofit boards.

The most common names for these bodies are board of directors or board of trustees. Other designations include board of governors or board of managers. Churches tend to have their own nomenclature, such as deacons, elders, or vestry.

Whatever the name, all have in common one purpose: Boards and board members are legally responsible, collectively and individually, for the actions of the nonprofit organizations they serve. The board holds its organization "in trust"; the organization is committed to the care of the board, and individual members are required to discharge their duties with care and diligence. The board is empowered to manage the funds and to decide the policy of a nonprofit organization.

Over the years I've accumulated quite a list of tasks a board performs. These often have been designated as "reasons" why boards are necessary.

- Act as trustee
- Function as court of last resort
- Insure financial solvency
- Approve long-range plans
- Determine goals and objectives
- Establish policies
- Attend meetings
- Determine mission
- Select and appoint executive director
- Read information
- Oversee management functions
- Provide governance
- Interpret organization to community
- Create bylaws
- Be legally accountable for agency operation
- Participate in organizational activities
- Approve budget
- Select and recruit board members
- Evaluate organization
- Vote on issues
- Serve on committees
- Raise money

We could continue in this fashion until the list became so lengthy that no one would remember or even read it. In fact, in some of my graduate classes we created lists that exceeded fifty items.

As I read and reread these lists and studied the literature, it seemed to me that all the tasks fell into three categories:

- Some of them were board decisions.
- Some of them were actions required of individual board members.
- Some of them were "behaviors" required of board members.

These three groupings suggested the designation of three corresponding categories to provide context for a discussion of "what a board is for." I designated these categories as follows:

- *Functions* of the board: What the board does collectively.
- *Roles* of the board member: What the individual board member does.
- *Behaviors* required to achieve maximum role and function effectiveness.

The making of policy is an example of a collective board function. Within that collective function, one important role of the individual board member is the casting of that member's vote in board meetings and in committee. One of the behaviors required of board members in order to achieve maximum role and function effectiveness is to be prepared by reading all information pertinent to the issues under debate. Function, role, and behavior will be discussed in subsequent chapters. Figure 4-1 provides a context for the board function or "what a board does."

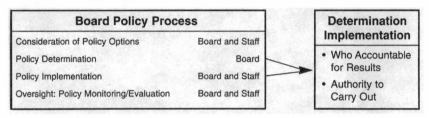

Figure 4-1. What a board does

In carrying out its duties, every board must observe two fundamental principles:

- A board of directors must act both legally and ethically.
- A board of directors can delegate, but it cannot abdicate its accountability for the results of that delegation.

Note that these principles require that "policy" be unambiguously defined, as it will be later in this book. There are two critical points that are often overlooked when policy is discussed. First, when a board makes a policy decision, it must be very clear who is to be held accountable for the implementation of that policy decision. Second, the board must be certain that the delegated party has the authority to carry out the policy. Both of these points will be discussed in subsequent chapters.

Section II

What a Board Is

5

Legal Implications of Serving on a Nonprofit Board of Directors

Every day the news media report that there is a suit being filed on behalf of an individual or a group for some injustice, real or imagined. There was a time when charitable organizations were exempt from legal actions. Unfortunately, that time is long past. Board members must be keenly aware of the legal liability they assume when they join a nonprofit organization. They can find themselves individually and collectively liable for significant sums of money through acts or omissions resulting from their own ignorance or negligence.

This still-painful incident happened to a client a few years ago. The organization in question was a relatively small community-based nonprofit. The Internal Revenue Service sent a letter informing the board that the organization had not filed quarterly withholding statements for the previous twelve quarters. The organization had suffered an income shortfall, and the staff had decided that the best way to deal with this problem was simply not to pay the IRS, imagining that the money owed could be made up later. Of course it never was. The executive director responsible for this decision had resigned and disappeared long before the arrival of the IRS letter.

The money owed, about $35,000, became the board's responsibility. The board and the IRS did reach an accommodation, however—each board member was assessed to pay a portion the bill. Not only had the board members failed to understand their legal accountability for actions taken by the organization, they had failed even to conduct oversight.

Boards must understand their legal responsibility and take appropriate steps to respond to legal action, if and when it is brought. The voluntary or nonprofit organization is a corporation. In legal terms, a for-profit or non-profit corporation is usually considered an entity separate and distinct from its members. It is a fictitious legal person afforded the same rights and subject to the same obligations as natural persons. As a fictitious person, however, the corporation itself cannot carry out those actions it is empowered to undertake by the state. The board volunteers, officers, and employees who are authorized to act for the corporation are the "agents" through which the corporation acts. The corporate form exists, in part, to limit the individual board volunteer's liability. The key word here is *limit*. It does not mean *negate*. Although the corporate form protects individuals from personal liability for corporate actions, every state has penalties for negligence.

The best protection is prevention. Prevention means that each board volunteer must carry out his or her responsibilities conscientiously, remain informed of operations, and retain legal counsel for advice.

Consider the Estes rule on directors' liability:

$$I_3-Se = Pm$$

That is, "Inquiry times Information times Involvement without Self-enrichment leads to Peace of Mind." The three I's offer an excellent guide for a board volunteer's behavior in performing this role.

Board volunteers must *inquire* to determine whether the information they are receiving is complete and accurate. Too many board volunteers accept reports or information without comment. This habit is passive. Without reliable *information*, no responsible decision can be made. Any information received is validated through active participation, or *involvement*, in the board volunteer role.

The Estes Rule subtracts *self-enrichment*, because voluntary organizations must be very careful to avoid conflicts of interest. Suits alleging a conflict of interest are among the strongest that can be brought against voluntary organizations. Organizations may avoid such conflicts by enforcing one of the following policies:

- No member of the board, staff, or organization as a whole may have *any* business transaction with the organization as a group.

or

- Transactions may take place, but only under specific conditions stated in the bylaws.

Here is a sample bylaw statement concerning permissible transactions:

CONFLICT OF INTEREST. Any possible conflict of interest on the part of a director shall be disclosed to the board. When any such interest becomes a matter of board action, the director in question shall not vote or use personal influence on the matter, and shall not be counted in the quorum for a meeting at which board action is to be taken on the interest. The director may, however, briefly state a position on the matter, and answer pertinent questions of board members. The minutes of all actions taken on such matters shall clearly reflect that these requirements have been met.

A transparent bidding procedure is also recommended, so that the bid of a board volunteer, if accepted, is clearly the best choice for the organization.

Prevention also means doing everything possible to reduce the likelihood of a suit being won and to discourage a suit from ever being brought. Nothing, however, can prevent a determined plaintiff from filing a suit. It is the responsibility of the diligent board member to understand this fact and to be prepared to defend the organization's interests when a suit is brought. The following are brief outlines of some types of protection from liability that may apply to nonprofit organizations:

- *Sovereign immunity* means that a state and its agencies are immune from suit without the state's consent.
- *Charitable immunity* is the concept that an organization "devoted to the public good" should be protected from legal liability. This doctrine has been abrogated by most state legislatures and is now, for all practical purposes, nonexistent.
- *Indemnification* means simply that an organization has assumed the obligation to pay or reimburse someone for loss or expense resulting from

a finding of legal liability. Individual state law must be reviewed to determine the applicability of indemnification agreements to voluntary organizations in a given jurisdiction.

- *Insurance* is a purchased form of indemnification. It is a policy covering an individual or class of individuals. Insurance, of course, may be purchased by an individual or by an organization on behalf of an individual.

Although reliance on legal counsel may not relieve a board volunteer of liability, the use of counsel can reduce the possibility of suit and a subsequent finding of liability. The attorney representing the organization should not be a board member but should be familiar with the organization.

Here's a short checklist of board procedures that may help to limit legal liability:

- Are notices of meetings mailed as required by the bylaws to prevent any claim that certain persons were intentionally excluded?
- Have the minutes of board meetings been certified by the secretary and approved by the Board? They are legal documents.
- Are motions clearly stated and votes recorded? Votes against any issue don't lessen liability, but a clear record of proceedings can be invaluable evidence in a trial or hearing.
- Are all local, state, and federal reports being prepared accurately and on time?
- Are budget reports and balance sheets distributed at regular intervals?
- Are all contracts current?
- Is the organization hiring qualified staff to deliver services?
- Are fund-raising costs reasonable?
- Are any land or money trusts legally supervised?
- Is legal counsel *not* on the board?
- Are board actions in compliance with the bylaws?
- Are the bylaws reviewed annually?
- Are audits conducted annually?
- Is the auditing firm *not* on the board?
- Are all federal, state, and local financial obligations current and on time?

In addition to the conflict of interest bylaw, here are two more bylaws for consideration:

Indemnification

Indemnification bylaws can take many forms, depending on local legal requirements. The following is only a sample. You should have an attorney draft an article that is tailored to local laws and the specific requirements of your organization.

1. ACTION BY OTHER THAN CORPORATION. The corporation shall indemnify any person who was or is a party or is threatened to be made a party to any threatened, pending, or completed action, suit or proceeding, whether civil, criminal, administrative or investigative (other than an action by or in the right of the corporation) by reason of the fact that such person is or was a director, or officer of the corporation, or is or was serving at the request of the corporation as a director or officer of another corporation, partnership, joint venture, trust or other enterprise, against expenses (including attorneys' fees), judgments, fines and amounts paid in settlement actually and reasonably incurred by such person in connection with such action, suit or proceeding if such person acted in good faith and in a manner which such person reasonably believed to be in or not opposed to the best interests of the corporation and with respect to any criminal action or proceeding had no reasonable cause to believe the conduct was unlawful. The termination of any action, suit or proceeding by judgment, order, settlement, conviction, or upon a plea of *nolo contendere* or its equivalent, shall not, of itself, create a presumption that the person did not act in good faith and in a manner which the person reasonably believed to be in or not opposed to the best interests of the corporation, and, with respect to any criminal action or proceeding, had reasonable cause to believe that the person's conduct was unlawful.

2. ACTION BY CORPORATION. The corporation shall indemnify any person who was or is a party or is threatened to be made a party to any threatened, pending or completed action or suit by or in the right of the corporation to procure a judgment in its favor by reason of the fact that such person is or was a director or officer of the corporation, or is or was serving at the request of the corporation as a director or officer of another corporation, partnership, joint venture, trust or other enterprise against expenses (including attorneys' fees) actually and reasonably incurred in connection with the defense or settlement of such action or suit if such person acted in good faith and in a manner such person reasonable believed to be in or not opposed to the best interests of the corporation and except that no indemnification shall be made in respect of any claim, issue or matter as to which such person shall have been adjudged to be liable for

willful negligence or misconduct in the performance of duty to the corporation unless and only to the extent that the court in which such action or suit was brought shall determine upon application that despite the adjudication of liability, but in view of all the circumstances of the case, such person is fairly and reasonably entitled to indemnity for such expenses which the court shall deem proper.

3. EXPENSES. To the extent that a director or officer has been successful on the merits or otherwise in defense of any action, suit or proceeding referred to in Sections 1 and 2 above, or in defense of any claim, issue or matter therein, such director or officer shall be indemnified against expenses (including attorneys' fees) actually and reasonably incurred in connection therewith.

4. PREREQUISITES. Any indemnification under Sections 1 and 2 above (unless ordered by a court) shall be made by the corporation only as authorized in the specific case upon a determination that indemnification of the director or officer is proper in the circumstances because the director or officer has met the applicable standard of conduct set forth in Section 1 and 2. Such determination shall be made (1) by the board by a majority vote of a quorum consisting of directors who were not parties to such action, suit or proceeding, or (2) if such a quorum is not obtainable, or, even if obtainable a quorum of disinterested directors so directs, by independent legal counsel in a written action.

5. ADVANCES BY CORPORATION. Expenses incurred in defending a civil or criminal action, suit or proceeding may be paid by the corporation in advance of the final disposition of such action, suit or proceeding as authorized by the board in the specific case upon receipt of an undertaking by or on behalf of the director or officer, to repay such amount unless it shall ultimately be determined that the director or officer is entitled to be indemnified by the corporation as authorized in this article.

6. OTHER REMEDIES. The indemnification provided by this article shall not be deemed exclusive of any other rights to which such director or officer may be entitled under any agreement, vote of disinterested directors or otherwise, both as to action in an official capacity and as to action in another capacity while holding such office, and shall continue as to a person who has ceased to be a director or officer, and shall inure to the benefit of the heirs, executors and administrators of such a person.

Insurance

Insurance bylaws, like indemnification bylaws, may take many forms. The following is only a sample. You should have an attorney draft an article that is tailored to local laws and the specific requirements of your organization.

> INSURANCE. The corporation may purchase and maintain insurance on behalf of any person who may be indemnified her against any liability asserted against such person and incurred in any capacity, or arising out of any status, for which the person may be indemnified.

The importance of these provisions is illustrated by a memorable case in which a social service agency and its board of directors were sued by a parent whose child allegedly had been abused by a staff member. The indemnification and insurance bylaws provided the basis for paying for the defense of the board members who were sued. Without these two articles, individual board members would have had to pay for their own defense.

Finally, there are many local organizations and individuals who can assist in determining the legal and insurance needs of a nonprofit. The following are three national organizations that may be of assistance:

Independent Sector
1200 Eighteenth St., NW
Suite 200
Washington, DC 20036
202–467–6100
Fax: 202–467–6101
www.independentsector.org

Alliance for Nonprofit Management
1899 L St., NW
6th Floor
Washington, DC 20036
202–955–8406
Fax: 202–955–8419
www.allianceonline.org

First Nonprofit Mutual Insurance Company
111 N. Canal St.
Suite 802
Chicago, IL 60606
800–526–4352
Fax: 312–930–0375
www.firstnonprofit.com

Other sources of information include local United Ways, bar associations, and the office of the secretary of state.

6

Committees

They have been called "the task force of democracy." It has been said that our democratic society could not function without them. These are high words of praise—clear indications of the critical role of committees. And yet, in every comedian's book of favorite jokes there is at least one about committees: "A camel is a horse put together by a committee." Clever speakers feel they must join the attack: "A committee is a group of the unfit trying to lead the unwilling to do the unnecessary." Board members snicker: "What committee did they stick you on?" Staff executives gripe: "I've got another committee meeting coming up. What am I going to do with it?" And finally, committees become the fear of anyone who is part of an organization: "Never make a suggestion—you'll be appointed to chair a committee to look into it." The paradox is obvious, the implications rather frightening.

The effectiveness of a board is measured by achievements of its committees, not by the board itself. The truth is that when we say our board is not functioning, we really mean our committees are not functioning. It is at the committee level that a board will succeed or fail. Every board member must be effectively involved at the committee level where the real work and the interaction (debate) take place. Whenever a committee recommendation comes before the board, it should already have had a thorough screening at

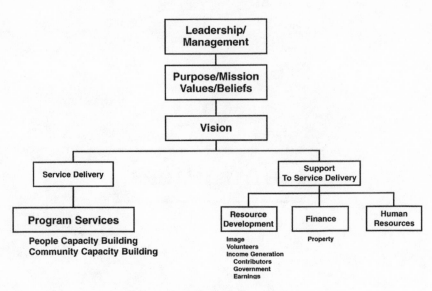

Figure 6-1. The Work to Be Done

the committee level. The board can then act upon the reports and recommendations of the committee. A committee need not put together a camel instead of a horse!

Where Do Committees Come From?

Anyone can draw up a list of committees, but it is more difficult to describe how they come about. In chapter 2, I introduced the concept of the "Work to Be Done." Whatever an organization perceives its work to be, it must construct its own version of the "Work to Be Done" chart illustrated in Figure 6-1.

As noted earlier, the "Work to Be Done" model has many applications. One of these applications is the establishment of committees within an organization, as illustrated in Figure 6-2.

In a small organization, the board may function as a committee of the whole, which means that the board handles *all* the work without committees. Slightly more complex organizations sometimes combine committees, such as program/human resources and development/finance. In still larger and more complex organizations, there may be four standing committees, or even a network of subcommittees, as illustrated in Figure 6-3.

THE WORK TO BE DONE TO STANDING COMMITTEES

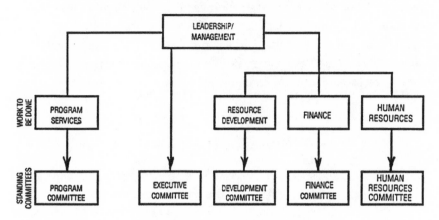

Figure 6-2. Standing committees

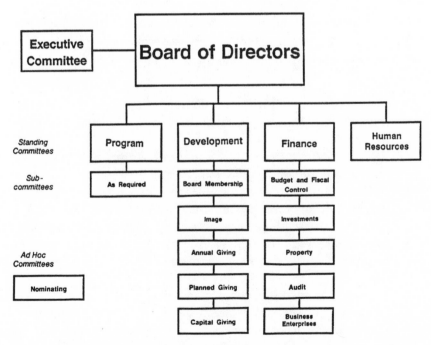

Figure 6-3. Standing committees and subcommittees

At all times, any committee must trace its origin back to some work the organization must accomplish. If a committee is formed that does not find its rationale for being in the work of an organization, there arises a logical question: What function does the committee serve? I once worked with the board of an organization that had a complicated structure of twenty-two committees. Using the "Work to Be Done" model as a template, this board discovered that it had thirteen committees whose function had been lost. This was a terrible waste of organizational energy.

What Do They Do?

Once the origin and structure of a committee are clear, we can examine how it should work. Later we will lay out the way boards plan to meet organizational objectives in greater detail. For the moment, let figure 6–4 serve as an outline of how committees get their "work" done. Within the "Work to Be Done" model, each individual task presents a set of goals and objectives that provide the basis of a committee's operation. A committee description sets the parameters of a committee's operation, while a manual of operation provides detailed information on how a committee achieves its work.

A successfully functioning committee must have the following ingredients:

- A *specific commission* is a definitive document clearly describing what the committee is to do. A specific commission permits committee members to know what they are doing and why.
- The key to an effective committee is an *effective chairperson.* He or she sets the tone and pace, and proposes strategies to the committee. The chairperson must be thoroughly acquainted with the organization's goals and the part the committee plays in their achievement. He or she delegates and coordinates work and maintains a climate for thoughtful deliberation. An effective chairperson is a "leader-enabler." The importance of this job and its objectives should be made clear before appointment of a chairperson.
- If the key to an effective committee is an effective chairperson, the key to an effective chairperson is an *effective staff executive.* He or she must work closely with the chairperson, assisting in the preparation of agendas and providing all the pertinent data required to operate an effective committee meeting.

A Committee's Work

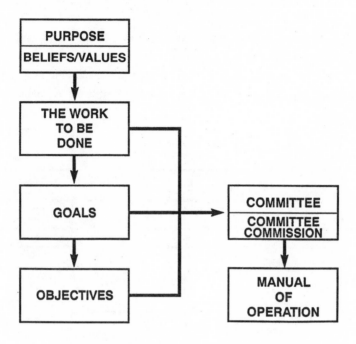

Figure 6–4. How a committee works

- *Effective committee meetings* generally result if the first three ingredients are present. Such meetings are action-oriented, based on a sound agenda, with all data necessary for decision-making at hand.
- *Committee members should be thoughtfully appointed,* with a clear view of the goals the committee must achieve and of the skills brought by each member to assist in the achievement of those goals.

When a new board member is recruited, it is best that he or she be told the proposed committee assignment at that time. A new board member will be immediately effective when serving on a committee that falls within his or her area of expertise. After at least one year of service, a new board volunteer should be able to serve on any committee of choice.

Committee Agenda Building and Meeting Review

When staff works directly with committees, executives often fear a loss of control and a lack of communication. This situation can be avoided through the agenda-building process and meeting review, as shown in Figure 6–5. The heart of any effective committee meeting, the agenda, is the product of a team effort between board and staff. The agenda is established through the following process: The executive director meets with the staff liaison to the

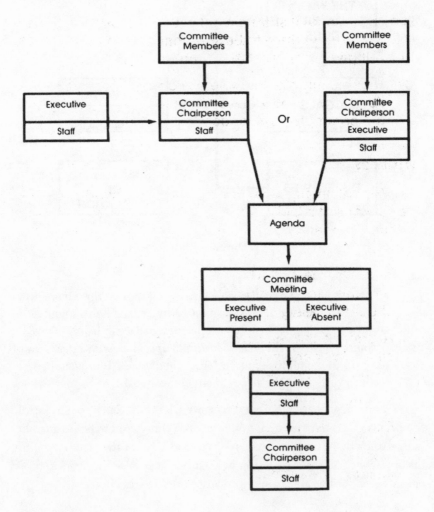

Figure 6–5. Committee agenda building and meeting review

NEWPORT ORGANIZATION

FINANCE COMMITTEE MEETING

April 10, 20_

A G E N D A

1. Approval of Agenda

2. Newport Organization Accounting Proposal

3. Review Investment of Current Bequests

4. Future Investments of Endowment Fund

5. Review of Current Cash Position and Cash-Flow Problem in June

6. Other Business

7. Adjournment

ATTENDING:

George L. Pierce, Chairman	Samuel L. Black
Thomas F. Adams	Executive Director
Herman L. Dent	
Harold P. Jefferson	Herbert R. Munsey
Sylvia N. Otterness	Director of Business Administration
Frank Prett	Jane L. Pryor
Carleton S. Rhodes	Associate Director
	of Business Administration

Figure 6–6. Sample agenda

committee. The staff liaison then meets with the committee chairperson. The final decision on the agenda belongs to the committee chairperson. Diplomacy must sometimes guide the staff liaison should the committee chairperson's decision run contrary to the wishes of the executive director. Of course, it is also possible for the executive and the staff liaison meet together with the committee chairperson to set the agenda. Figure 6–6 shows a sample finance committee agenda, and Figure 6–7 outlines one possible format for reviewing an agenda item. Be sure to mail these materials well in advance of the meeting.

The actual committee meeting can now be held with or without the presence of the executive. Afterward, the executive and the staff liaison should meet to discuss the outcome. It is also helpful for the staff liaison to meet with the committee chairperson to review the meeting.

NEWPORT ORGANIZATION

FINANCE COMMITTEE MEETING

April 10, 20__

AGENDA ITEM # 2

Situation:

Beginning July 1, 20__, all reporting is to be based on cost accounting principles, requiring all items of income and expense to be classified into programs and activities with their related statistics. At present, our system does not provide for the collection of this data.

Blodgett & Co. was engaged to design a system for the collection and reporting of this information in order to satisfy the new requirements as well as to provide a management tool for internal control. This system was presented to our computer firm for a peliminary estimate of the costs of developing and operating the system on an annual basis. Their proposal is attached.

Conversion costs from the present system, for both fund accounting and payroll function, will be approximately $5,000, bringing the total set-up costs to around $27,400. Monthly payroll processing under the new system will be around $500 per month, or $6,000 per year, bringing the total annual operating costs to approximately $34,200. These costs are based on estimates, since the volume of transactions under the new system was unknown.

Options:

Based on the above information, several options are available:

1. Implement entire system with full operation beginning July 1, 20__ .

2. Implement entire system, but omit budget input, resulting in reports containing actual figures only. This would delete the control factor and leave interpretation of results questionable.

3. Delay implementation of system. This would require the hiring of *at least* two additional staff persons in order to gather and formulate manually the data necessary for Community Fund reporting.

Recommendation: It is the belief of the Administrative staff that this system, while providing the necessary information for reporting, will also serve as a tool for internal control in analyzing the cost effectiveness and organizational equity of all programs, and we recommend that the Committee approve the proposal as outlined in Option #1.

Action Required: Review the proposal and available options, and make a recommendation to the Board of Directors.

Figure 6-7. Sample agenda item review format

Minutes

Minutes are crucial to committee work, but are seldom done well, if done at all. Although their necessity isn't always immediately obvious, minutes serve as reference materials for any questions which may arise about committee actions. Because the person who takes minutes does not have an opportunity to participate fully, a competent staff secretary should be assigned to that task. A draft of the minutes should be reviewed by the responsible staff person and approved by the board or committee secretaries before distribution. This should happen no later than one week after the meeting. Nowadays, minutes are distributed by e-mail, and full sets of minutes are easily saved for reference.

Minutes should be concise and complete, of course. All committee reports should be attached to ensure accurate reporting. It also helps if each person who makes a motion jots down his or her own wording for the benefit of exact recording. In summary, there should be a set format for minutes. It should correspond to the agenda.

In reality, only two things take place in committee or board meetings: 1) communication, or passing on helpful information; and 2) decisions. Both should be either included in the minutes or attached to it. All communication items should be attached, not integrated into the minutes. Decision items need to report only three things: the decision made, the responsibility assigned for follow-up, and any action deadlines. A review of discussions is futile; they are difficult to write, time-consuming to read, and add little value to the decision made. Figure 6–8 is a useful format for minutes of committee meetings, and may also be applied to minutes of board meetings.

Committee Composition

In the appointment of committee members, it is important to note that committee membership does not necessarily require board membership. Many boards increase involvement by including nonboard members. Many require that the committee chairpersons be board members, but this really doesn't matter. Committees may include consultants with specific skills that broaden those of the board. Construction people, for example, could serve on the property committee, advertising people on the public relations committee, educators on the program services committee, and so on. It is

NEWPORT ORGANIZATION

PROGRAM SERVICES COMMITTEE MEETING

April 17, 20___

MINUTES

ATTENDING:

Lester B. Cannon, Chairperson
Franklin Byman
Gordon Fletcher
Juanita Perez
Clifton Rhodes
Mary Wilson

William H. Logan, Program
　Director
Louis Bend, Group Work
　Supervisor
Herbert L. Munsey, Director
　Business Administration

Agenda Item	Communication Attached	DECISION		
		Decision	Responsi-bility for follow-up	Deadline
2. Program Service Report	X			
3. Review of Statistics	X			
4. Request for individual tutoring		yes—6 no—0	W.H. Logan	Report progress in one month
5. Progress report on Teen Center	X			
6. Review of 20___ budget process and role of Program Services Committee	X			

Figure 6-8. Sample minute format

important that if a person is asked to serve on a committee, he or she be allowed a vote, board member or not. Some organizations give the vote only to board volunteers; nonboard members should at least be made individual advisors if a vote is not to be given.

Ad Hoc Committees

Ad hoc committees are short-duration committees formed to accomplish a specific task. There must be a clear differentiation between ad hoc and standing committees. Standing committees deal with the *ongoing processes* of an organization. They are concerned with system maintenance and evaluation. Ad hoc committees are formed to research, study, evaluate, or solve problems. Ad hoc committees should be of predetermined duration. They can be formed either from within a specific committee or by appointing members from any or all of the committees of the board. Ad hoc committees should also be able to elicit participation from outside the board and committee structure of the organization. They should always have a clear commission outlining what they should accomplish.

Committee Commissions

"May I see the job description?" is probably one of the first requests made by staff executives when interviewing for a new position. A clear job description is absolutely necessary if the candidate is to understand the requirements of the position. Curiously, the staff often asks board volunteers to accept responsibilities without giving them any clear definition of the requirements. Committees, too, may be asked to function without any explanation of what is expected of them. Just as the staff requires job descriptions, so do committees. Committee job descriptions—known as "commissions"—should have three basic components:

General commission:	A broad statement of the purpose of the committee.
Appointments and composition:	How appointments are made and who serves on each committee.
Responsibilities:	A definite description of the activities required of the committee.

However responsibilities are written, they must relate directly back to the organization's Work to Be Done.

Manuals of Operation

Manuals of operation are constructed to assist a committee in the accomplishment of its tasks. They contain procedures and forms which are useful to both board members and staff. See chapter 14 for an example of this type of document.

Parliamentary Procedure

Parliamentary procedure is a very useful means for the chairperson of a meeting to ensure the orderly and efficient conduct of business. Parliamentary procedure also provides for discipline, when necessary, of participants in a meeting. For example, I recall a certain individual who constantly interrupted the flow of business by wanting to discuss items already closed or by bringing up information not germane to the discussion. Parliamentary procedure can control these and many other situations. There is a real danger, however, that the participants may become so concerned with procedure that the substance of the meeting is lost. *Robert's Rules of Order,* perhaps the best-known compendium of parliamentary procedure, is a very cumbersome book. There are, however, abbreviated versions of the rules of parliamentary procedure. One such version, in both Spanish and English, may be ordered from:

Voluntary Management Press
4800 Prince
Downers Grove, IL 60515
Phone: 630–964–0432
Fax: 630–964–7501
E-mail: billconrad2@attbi.com
Website: www.ifvo.org

The Value of Committees

A well-known industrialist once said this of committees: "If you want to kill any idea in the world today, get a committee working on it." By contrast, a committee member at a recent conference spoke expansively of their value, claiming that all organizational ills would be reduced to mere minor nuisances if only we were to make good use of committees. The ideal, of course, lies somewhere in between these two extremes. In practice, committees

- Recommend new items or changes to the action goals and objectives under their jurisdiction to the board of directors;
- Monitor the result of the action goals and objectives when approved by the board of directors;
- Coordinate activities with the other committees through the executive committee.

They are the basic action elements of voluntarism.

Here is one final point about committees. Many organizations use committees as a training ground for new board volunteers. In these organizations, individuals cannot be elected to the board of directors unless they have served well as a committee member. This is a healthy mechanism for maintaining a high level of involvement and should be given serious consideration.

7

Function and Composition
of the Executive Committee

For many years, it was an accepted practice in the business world to combine two key tasks into one position, that of chairman of the board. The chairman headed the board, of course, but also headed the employees. Most members of the board of directors were *"inside" directors*. This term refers to members of the board who are also employees of the business. This situation set up an inherent conflict of interest. It is difficult to serve on a board and maintain an independent point of view when the chairman of the board is also your employees' boss.

Interestingly, in recent years corporate America has adopted the nonprofit model of leadership, splitting the responsibilities of the old chairman's position. Today, the chairperson heads the board, while the president is designated chief executive officer (CEO) and heads the employees. The officers of the board of directors often take on classic designations like chairperson or president of the board, vice chairpersons or vice presidents, secretary, and treasurer. Committees are often fitted out with their own lists of positions and titles.

It is a standard operating procedure in most nonprofit organizations for

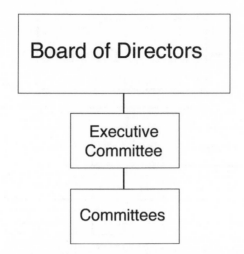

Figure 7-1. Executive committee—ineffective method of organization

the officers of the board to be designated to serve on the executive committee. Most state laws governing nonprofit organizations describe what an executive committee is and what it does. Some articles describing executive committee composition and function are a few paragraphs long, while others may run on for ten or more pages. There is, however, one common thread: an executive committee has legal status and can commit the entire board to a course of action decided by that executive committee. The entire board is legally responsible for the actions of its executive committee.

Accordingly, there should be an article in the bylaws describing the function and composition of the executive committee. Remember also that the larger the board of directors is, the more influential the executive committee becomes. Often executive committees become so powerful that board meetings become nothing more than pro forma approval of executive committee decisions. This tendency must be guarded against. The primary function of the executive committee is to act in emerging situations when the entire board cannot be brought into session. Any decisions made by the executive committee must be discussed at the next board meeting, and the full board has the authority to overturn my executive committee decision with which it disagrees.

Any prohibitions on actions by the executive committee should be noted in the bylaws. For example, the executive committee should not be allowed to change the budget; to retain, evaluate, or dismiss the executive director; to enter into any contracts on behalf of the board of directors; to

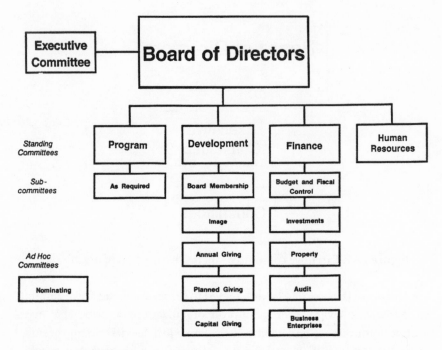

Figure 7–2. Executive committee—more effective method of organization

dispose of organizational assets; to represent the organizational publicly; to appoint or dismiss board officers or board members; or to modify board-approved policies. The bylaws should also provide for exceptions to these rules upon the direct approval of the board of directors.

The executive committee should direct the strategic planning process. There is no need for a separate strategic planning committee. An effective, functioning executive committee should have ample time to oversee the strategic planning process. Executive committees often act as screeners or checkers of committee reports that are to go before the board. This is an enormous waste of time. If the organization has properly conducted the agenda-building process outlined in chapter 6, a committee should report directly to the board, not to the executive committee. Nor is it desirable to make individual committees responsible to the executive committee; such a relationship short-circuits committee accountability to the board of directors and enhances the power and influence of the executive committee.

Figure 7–2 depicts a more desirable method of organization, one in which both the committees and the executive committee report to the board of directors. This arrangement better illustrates the actual functions of the executive committee, the committees, and the board of directors.

Because the executive committee has such influence and power potential, the committee's composition must be carefully analyzed. A typical executive committee is composed of officers, such as the chairperson or president, secretary, and treasurer; it usually does not include the committee chairs. This means that the board members most familiar with the operations of the organization do not serve on the executive committee. When issues come before the executive committee which require action, the people most familiar with those issues are not present unless specifically invited. A better model might include the chairpersons of various committees as vice presidents or vice chairpersons of the executive committee. Each organization, however, must make its own decisions based on its size, complexity, and purpose.

8

Roles, Functions, and Relations of Board and Staff

The Function of the Board and Staff: What They Do as a Group

What does a board do? In chapter 4, I touched upon the concepts of function, role, and behavior as they relate to boards and board members. Let us return to these themes in more detail. A casual survey of the literature suggests that boards act as trustees and courts of last resort, insure financial solvency, approve long-range plans, determine goals and objectives, establish policies, determine missions, select and appoint executive directors, oversee management functions, provide governance, interpret their organizations to the community, write bylaws, provide legal accountability for their operations, approve budgets, select and recruit board members, and evaluate their organizations.

Long ago, it occurred to me that understanding the function of a board simply by drawing up such a list was the wrong approach. By combining sets of different, but related, activities into a single list, the relationships between the sets and between the individual activities would be lost. Better, I thought, to group these activities according to the *function* of the board, the *role* of its members, and the *behaviors* required of those members for effective stewardship. Before further discussion of these concepts, we would do well to remember several key principles.

Boards have authority only when a quorum is present. The only exception to this rule is called *unanimous consent,* meaning that action can be taken without a meeting if a written consent is given by all of the directors entitled to a vote.

No individual board member has the authority to commit the organization, give instructions to employees, or represent the board without an express mandate from the board of directors.

By law, all board members share responsibility for governance of the institution. Therefore, all members must be afforded the opportunity to speak, and should be encouraged to share their experience. It is the responsibility of the chairperson to conduct meetings in such a way as to ensure that all board members have an equal opportunity for full participation.

Similarly, all board members must have equal access to all information relevant to the exercise of their responsibility. Board members have an obligation to keep themselves informed, just as trustees or corporate directors do.

Board members must be given the opportunity to take part in meaningful activities, such as serving on task forces and committees, giving speeches and interviews, and so on.

Board members must place the larger interests of the organization above personal or factional concerns.

Staff must recognize the partnership they enjoy with the board, and should not view this relationship as burdensome or adversarial.

Board members and staff must, at all times, act legally and ethically.

The Board Function

Boards determine the general direction of the work to be done by the organization. More specifically, they consider policy options, determine policy, implement selected policies, perform oversight of organization operations (monitoring and evaluating), and serve as courts of last resort.

The Staff Function

The staff participates in and supports the board policy process, supports the board in implementation of selected policies, and implements board policies for which the chief staff officer is held accountable

The Role of Board and Staff Members: What They Do as Individuals

The following are *minimal* levels of role involvement, meaning *all* board members should play *all* of the following roles in *all* nonprofit organizations. Further expansion of these roles will depend upon the specific needs of the organization.

Board Member Role

I. Board policy process

The individual board member participates in the board policy process by casting his or her one vote. (Note that each board member actually has two votes: one at the committee level, when an issue is before the committee(s) on which the board member serves, and the other at the board level.) No individual board member can make policy.

II. Implementation

A. Resource Development

Image

Board members are important image-makers for the organization. A well-informed, committed board member is one of an organization's greatest image-making resources. Uninformed or uncommitted board members often contribute to a negative image.

Board Recruitment

Each board member helps identify new prospects for board membership. Each member should occasionally participate in the recruitment and orientation of new board members.

Support

Each board member is expected to participate in fund-raising. Board members should set personal fund-raising goals based on an individual contribution (or company contribution, where appropriate) and asking prospects for contributions. Personal goals should be set individually on an annual basis.

B. Sanction and Linkage

Sanction

By serving on a board of directors, board members signal that they believe the organization is a legitimate, difference-making organization. This does not always mean agreement on every issue, but it does mean that each board member must support policy decisions while he or she remains a member of the board.

Linkage

Board members bring an extraordinary wealth of knowledge about the community to board deliberations; they are among the most effective means of communicating with the community.

C. Staff Relationships

Chief Staff Officer

The board of directors has several responsibilities to the chief staff officer (CSO). An organization may use a search committee to conduct hiring; the vote to hire a CSO, however, is the responsibility of the entire board. The chairperson should initiate performance evaluations of the CSO; final evaluations, however, should be according to a vote of the entire board. As long as the CSO is on staff, the board must support its CSO. If the board can no longer summon this confidence, it probably needs a new CSO.

In my description of the four areas of fundamental agreement for any functioning board of directors and the board/staff relationship, I said that there was near unanimity on what constitutes the most important policy decision a board makes—retaining the chief staff officer. As crucial as this decision may be, it is second in importance to the performance assessment of the CSO. A board must regularly review the performance of its CSO to ensure that the CSO remains effective. Yet, in most boards I deal with, the performance assessment process for the CSO has ranged from nonexistent to superficial. For a useful instrument, obtain the Performance Assessment of the Staff Chief Executive from:

Voluntary Management Press
4800 Prince St.
Downers Grove, IL 60515
Phone: (630) 964-0432
Fax: (630) 964-7510
e-mail: billconrad2@attbi.com
website: www.ifvo.org

Staff

An effective and supportive board/staff relationship is essential to the effectiveness of the organization. Boards and committees have a right to expect timely, accurate, and substantial assistance from staff members. All board requests for information should be made through the chairperson to the CSO. All committee requests should go through the committee chairperson to the staff. Individual board member requests should go to appropriate staff members. Care must be taken, however, not to overwhelm staff with requests that are too extensive in scope or too marginal in value relative to the time and effort involved in fulfilling them. The CSO is the chief liaison to the board of directors. Board members should feel free to make suggestions to staff.

III. Advocacy

There will be times when board members will be asked to act as advocates for the organization. This can mean speaking on behalf of the organization, attending a meeting as part of a delegation, or writing a letter in furtherance of some organizational goal.

IV. Participation in Monitoring and Evaluation Process

All board members are expect to participate in two monitoring and evaluation processes conducted via the board of directors' self-assessment.

The behavior expected of board members is best spelled out from the first with a formalized invitation to service, a document containing basic information about the board of directors and the organization. The invitation should personalized with the name of the prospective member and should be issued immediately upon extension of the offer to join the organization. Here's an example:

Newport Organization Board of Directors
Commitment To Serve

I, _____, recognizing the important role I am undertaking as a member of the board of directors of the Newport Organization, hereby personally pledge to fulfill, in a diligent manner, all responsibilities inherent in my role as a board member.

My Role

I acknowledge the function of the board of directors and my role as a board member stipulated in my copy of the invitation to service. I understand that it will take four to six hours monthly to fulfill my role effectively.

My Commitment

I pledge:

1. To agree to serve on at least one committee or task force, attend all meetings, and participate in the accomplishment of its objectives;
2. To establish a high priority on my attendance at all meetings of the board and the committees and task forces on which I serve;
3. To come prepared to contribute to the discussion of issues and business to be addressed at scheduled meetings, having read the agenda and all background support material relevant to the meeting;
4. To observe the parliamentary procedures outlined in the *Condensed Parliamentary Procedure;*
5. To avoid conflicts of interest between my position as a board member and my personal and business life. If such a conflict does arise, I will declare that conflict before the board, and refrain from voting or discussing matters in which I have a conflict;
6. To support all actions taken by the board of directors, even when I am in a minority position on such actions;
7. To represent the Newport Organization in a supportive manner at all times and in all places;
8. To honor confidentiality;
9. To refrain from intruding in administrative issues that are the responsibility of staff, except as required to exercise my oversight role;
10. To participate in all board development programs designed to enhance the effectiveness of my performance as a board member, and to participate in the annual board self-assessment process;
11. To visit the Newport Organization facilities on a regular basis;
12. To read all Newport Organization publications;
13. To treat the Newport Organization's affairs as I do my own personal and business affairs;
14. To monitor the activity of the executive committee to insure it does not overstep its authority;
15. To fulfill commitments within agreed-upon deadlines;
16. To provide easy access to staff by phone or visitation;
17. To be sensitive to staff's organizational problems and to recognize organizational and long-term consequences of ideas and policies;
18. To refrain from asking a staff person to render an opinion about his or her colleagues, the Newport Organization, or other board members;

19. To notify staff if I have changed my mind with regard to a position taken in a private meeting, before going to the public with this changed position;
20. To devote my full attention to the discussion during a meeting with a staff person; and,
21. To recognize the achievements of staff.
22. If, for any reason, I am unable to fulfill any of the above commitments, I will discuss the issue with the chairperson of the board of directors and will resign from the board of directors if appropriate.

Date_____

Signed_____

Staff Member Role

The key role for staff with respect to its board is that of an *enabler*. The staff backs up the board and allows it to perform its functions effectively and efficiently. Enabling means providing a cause to believe in, a framework within which to work, lists of specific tasks to be accomplished (with deadlines), and opportunity for participation in the decisions that affect the first four.

To be effective, every board volunteer must be proud of the voluntary organization he or she serves. The board volunteer must be able to identify with the purpose of the organization and to represent it, when necessary, with confidence and conviction. During the recruitment process, a board volunteer usually asks, "Where do I fit?" or, in other words, "What is the framework within which I must work?" The volunteer wants to know precisely his or her place in the organizational structure and operations of the nonprofit organization. Invariably, the next question is, "What do you want me to do?" It is important that staff be very clear about these tasks and bear in mind definite deadlines for carrying them out.

The implication of these questions is that the staff is the source of all information for board volunteers. If, in fact, this happens, a board or committee will merely follow the lead of the staff, giving only superficial attention to the issues of the organization. Providing an opportunity to participate in decision-making is key. It is crucial that board volunteers have an opportunity to discuss issues if they are to remain engaged.

A board volunteer once said to me, "Don't ask me what I think—ask me what I think about what you think, then we'll get something done."

The message from the board volunteer to the staff member is clear: Do your homework. Come to me with data and your conclusions. I'll add mine, and we'll get the job done.

Board volunteers take initiative from staff initiative. They are only as effective as staff wishes or helps them to be; rarely do boards take over and actually lead day-to-day operations of the voluntary organization. In the words of another board volunteer, "God help us if the board decides to take the initiative all the time."

The subject of staff professionalism is a much-debated topic within voluntary organizations. The discussion usually centers on the mastery of a prescribed body of knowledge or on a set of professional degrees. Degrees are fine and, in many cases, necessary; but to board volunteers, their importance is secondary to that of simple competence and conscientiousness. Board volunteers are successful only to the extent that they are supported by staff. Let a staff member fail to return a phone call, provide inaccurate or late information, or embarrass a board volunteer, and all the knowledge and degrees in the world will not do any good. Board volunteers expect competence and personal integrity from their staff. They expect performance to keep pace with promises. They expect satisfaction with both direction and pace of work. Staff must remember, too, that board volunteers expect reasoned responses, not mere guesses or expressions of opinion Most of all, board volunteers should be able to predict the behavior of their staff. Consistency is the key. It can be useful to have an explicit, written contract between the staff and board:

Staff Commitment to the Board of Directors

    I, _____, recognizing the important role I play in the effectiveness of my board of directors, hereby personally pledge to fulfill, in a diligent manner, all responsibilities inherent in that role.

My Role

    I acknowledge the function of staff and my role as a staff member stipulated in my copy of the invitation to service.

My Commitment

    I pledge:

    1. To do my homework, and not to expect board members to take initiative in a vacuum;

2. To make working with the board an integral part of my work;
3. To refrain from using my board relationships to air organizational complaints or to advance a personal agenda;
4. To understand the difference between staff and board function, staff and board roles, policy and implementation and to work within the scope of my function and role;
5. To think and to plan in terms of results, not activities;
6. To respond promptly to phone calls;
7. To avoid embarrassing a board member in public meetings through inaccurate or insufficient data;
8. To respond to board member requests for data in a timely manner;
9. To refrain from manipulating information or board members in order to achieve a desired decision;
10. To ask for an appointment as follows:
    To call board members myself, not using a secretary as an intermediary;
    To meet with board members in their offices, whenever possible;
    To state the purpose of the meeting and the amount of time required;
    To take an agenda;
    To stick to the agenda and the time scheduled unless the board member alters them;
11. To be candid, but to respect appropriate confidentiality;
12. To meet agreed-upon deadlines, with adequate advance notification if deadlines cannot be met;
13. To prepare board members for meetings in which they must play a leadership role;
14. To recognize achievements of board members.

Date_____

Signed_____

To be remembered by staff:

> Value
> To say I volunteer
> For lack of something better to do
> Is to say my time has no value
> To say I volunteer
> Therefore, I work for you for nothing
> Is to say the work is worthless
> But to say

I choose to give my time to your work
Is to say
We both have value

—Lorraine Jensen

The Organization of the Board of Directors and the Board-Staff Relationship

Now that we have discussed organizational frameworks and the two principal actors, we are left with the following question: "How does it all go together?" Let's consider a model for board-staff cooperation and work.

I have an exercise for this part of the training or class session. I give each participant a small envelope with five cards. One card is labeled "Board of Directors"; three are labeled "Staff Members"; and the final card is labeled "Executive Director." I ask the members of the group to arrange the cards into a structure. It only takes a minute or two for each participant to arrange the cards.

This is the classic depiction of a board, useful because it clearly identifies the accountability of the board of directors and the executive

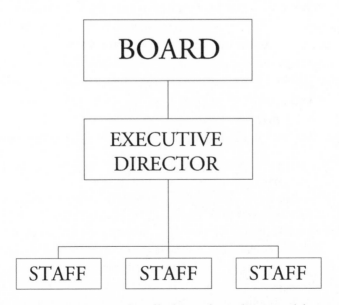

Figure 8-1. Board-staff relationship—classic model

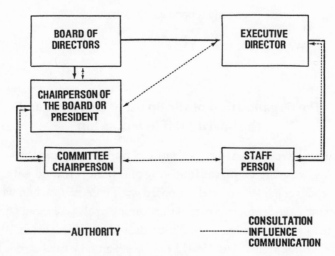

Figure 8-2. Board-staff relationship—revised model

director and establishes a legal framework. It doesn't, however, show the relationships between the staff and the board, the executive and board members, the operations or accountability of committees, or the responsibilities of staff assigned to those committees. Perhaps it would be better to abandon this model and to create a new one, beginning by identifying the board of directors, the board chairperson, and the executive director.

At this point, I give the participants a second envelope that contains four cards: one labeled "Chief Board Officer," and three labeled "Committee Chair." I then ask the group to create another model—one using all the cards—to depict the relationships. There are a number of creative models offered. Then, I distribute Figure 8-2.

There are several important points to note about this revised model:

1. The board of directors appoints, supervises, and evaluates the executive director.
2. The executive director works *with* the board chairperson or president, but does not *report* to him or her; neither does the board chairperson or president supervise the work of the executive director. This is to insure that the executive director is not *captured* by the board chairperson or president. The board can certainly assign some oversight responsibilities to the board chairperson or president, but these should be reviewed every three months in order to gauge the effectiveness of the work relationship they have established.

3. The executive director retains staff members who may be assigned committee responsibilities as required. The relationship of the committee chairperson and staff members should mirror that of the board chairperson and executive director. The staff member should work *with* the committee chairperson, but should not report to him or her.

Figure 8–3 illustrates the overall effect of the relationships set up according to our new model. I call this the *Leadership/Management Square.*

Within the Leadership/Management Square, the executive director designates which staff members will be responsible to work with each committee. The chairperson of the board selects and recruits his or her committee chairpersons. The staff person responsible for the committee should also accompany the chairperson or president in the recruiting process. This will solidify the relationship. (Note that the executive director need not join.)

The relationship between the chairperson and the executive director is illustrated by a dotted line. This indicates that the executive director reports to the board, not to the chairperson. The chairperson has the authority to assure that the will of the board is being carried out, but has no more independent authority than any other board volunteer. In his or her relationship with the executive director, the chairperson may request information and reports, set meetings and agendas, and decide how to handle issues within the board. The chairperson has no authority, however, to direct the executive director to implement a board policy that has been delegated to the executive director in a manner dictated by the chairperson. Implementation of board policy is solely the executive's prerogative in this instance. Policy implementation is difficult; it will not succeed without a clear operating framework and an atmosphere of trust among all parties.

It is particularly destructive for the executive director to go to committee members or other board volunteers in an attempt to manipulate the chairperson. It is equally destructive for the chairperson to go to the staff for information or opinions about the executive director. If the chairperson and the executive director cannot work out their differences, the board is the final arbiter.

All the good will and lateral organization in the world will not prevent problems from arising. However, good will and lateral organization can provide an environment conducive to solving problems and preventing

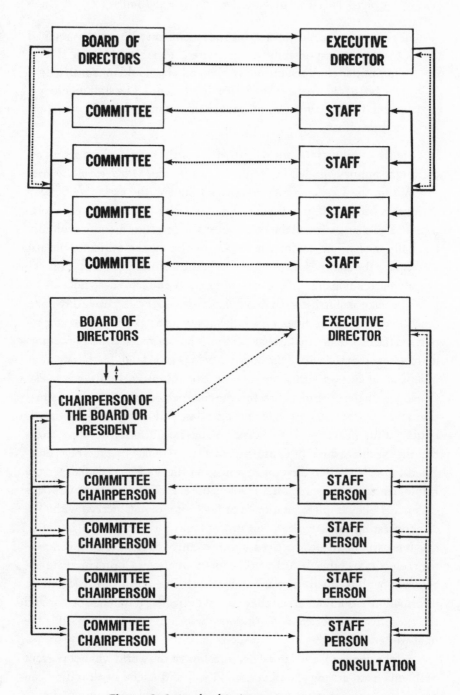

Figure 8-3. Leadership/Management Square

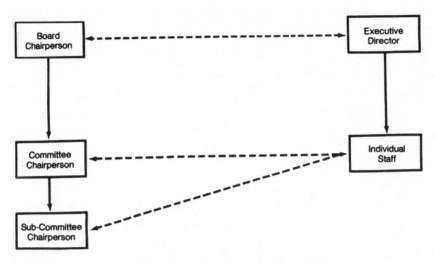

Figure 8–4. Problem-solving framework

them from evolving into crises. Figure 8–4 illustrates a problem-solving framework based on the Leadership/Management Square.

Accountability and Problem Solving

Problem:	Resolution:
Committee chairperson dissatisfied with individual staff.	Committee chairperson discusses problem with board chairperson. The committee chairperson then contacts the executive director. Sometimes the board chairperson will accompany to resolve issue.
Individual staff member dissatisfied with committee chairperson.	Individual staff member discusses problem with executive director. Both go to committee chairperson to resolve problem.
Subcommittee chairperson dissatisfied with the individual staff member.	The subcommittee chairperson consults with committee chairperson. If it cannot be handled at that end it moves to Step #1.
Staff member dissatisfied with subcommittee chairperson.	If it cannot be resolved at this end, it moves to Step #2.
Chairperson and/or executive director dissatisfied with the others.	The issue is resolved at the Board of Directors level.

The foregoing chart is for organizations that have no internal units and that have a board of directors separate from the governing board. There are, however, many organizations that have units with boards of their own. Leading and managing an organization of this type is very complex, and establishing clear relationships is of critical importance. The Leadership/Management Square is very useful in this case. The square cannot be expanded horizontally; however, it can be expanded vertically to accommodate any number of layers.

Figure 8–5 shows a Leadership/Management Square for a multi-unit organization.

To distinguish the different levels of boards, I refer to the legal board as the board of directors and the unit boards as board of managers.

The board of directors is the legal body vested with responsibility for operating the corporation in accordance with state laws, as designated in the corporate constitution and bylaws. The management of individual unit operations is delegated to boards of managers. The specifics of this delegated responsibility and authority should be clearly stated in the bylaws; this is the effective commission to the boards of managers to act on behalf of the

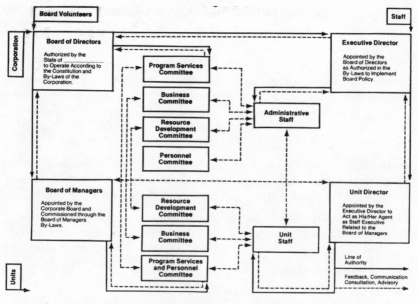

Figure 8–5. Leadership/Management Framework for a multi-unit organization

board of directors. The board of managers, in turn, organizes itself through an appropriate committee structure and presents each committee with its own written commission in an orderly delegation of responsibility.

In this example, the board of directors has four standing committees. In the unit structure, however, the personnel committee is integrated with the program services committee. Personnel (or human resources) issues are, in reality, concerns at the organizational level. The personnel function at the unit level is primarily in the program services area and is therefore integrated with that committee. This parallel organization facilitates communication and project implementation.

The program services, resource development, business, and personnel committees under the board of directors are committees for the organization as a whole, not for the board alone. Policy recommendations for board action come through these committees.

Periodically, the chairpersons of the standing committees at the organizational level should meet with their counterparts at the unit level for feedback, communications, advice, consultation, and training.

The only staff member directly responsible to the board is the executive director. Administrative staff members are responsible to their committee chairpersons and committees on a "dotted-line" basis. The unit directors are not responsible to their boards—they are responsible to the executive director. If conflict arises, conflict resolution moves up the two sides of the organization in parallel. If the executive director cannot resolve the conflict between a unit board of managers and the unit director, the board of directors becomes responsible for effecting a resolution.

In our example, the chairperson of the board of managers is represented on the board of directors and on the executive committee, ensuring that the voice of the units will be heard officially. It bears repeating that the chairpersons of the standing committees of the board of directors should meet periodically with their counterparts of the board of managers, maintaining a high level of communication between the corporation and its units.

The board volunteer-staff relationship must be based on a clear recognition, understanding, and acceptance of their respective roles, and organizations must be governed through board policy.

Section III

What a Board Does

9

A Systems Approach

What is a system? For our purposes, let's define it as an orderly arrangement of independent activities and related procedures that implement and facilitate the performance of an organization. This definition is quite a mouthful, but systems are neither new nor startling in their fundamentals. Almost all life is a system—our bodies certainly are. Our homes and universities are systems, as are our government agencies and our businesses. Each of these discrete systems holds within itself a number of subsystems, and has its own interconnections with various other systems that lie outside its borders. No one can, or should, disregard the way in which the components of any company, department, problem, technique, or program form a network with other systems.

A German biologist, Ludwig Von Bertalanffy, puts this another way in his *General Systems Theory.* According to this theory, all nature, including human behavior, is interconnected. Nothing can be understood in isolation; everything must be seen as part of a system. He hypothesized that it is a characteristic of nature to put things together in ever more synergistic and meaningful patterns and that each variable in a system interacts with the other variables so thoroughly that cause and effect cannot be separated.

A system is more than the sum of its parts; it must viewed as a whole. A nonprofit organization, like any other system, is made up of subsystems. The board of directors is a subsystem of the organization. Committees are subsystems of the board. The organization itself is a subsystem of the local community. The board must not only be aware of itself—it must be aware of all the subsystems of which it is composed and of all the larger systems of which it forms a part. To think this way is counter-intuitive to some, especially to those who have been educated according to linear models: B follows A, C follows B, and so on. Trying to work, think, and act holistically is a very different exercise. A system must be viewed as in dynamic homeostasis (homeostasis being a state of physiological equilibrium within an organism). Our bodies, for example, maintain constant temperature in the face of a changing environment.

The first to understand corporate management in the context of systems was New Jersey Bell Telephone Company president Chester I. Barnard. Writing over four decades ago, Barnard saw the executive as a component of a formal organization, and the organization as part of a larger cooperative system involving physical, biological, social, and psychological elements. Barnard's inclusion of physical and biological, as well as social and psychological, elements in the system in which the manager operates is perhaps a more accurate portrayal of the managerial subsystem than that expressed by most social psychologists, who view this subsystem as being related only to the social system. To be sure, most of a manager's interactions with others will involve social and psychological forces or elements. It is difficult, however, to exclude the manager's interactions with other elements, particularly with physical ones such as money, materials, and facilities.

In Barnard's classic 1938 book, *The Functions of the Executive,* he discussed cooperation as being critical to an effective organization:

> My purpose is first to provide a comprehensive theory of cooperative behavior in formal organizations. Cooperation originates in the need of an individual to accomplish purposes to which he is by himself biologically unequal. With the enlistment of other individuals, cooperation speedily becomes a constantly changing *system* made up of interrelated biological, psychological, and social elements. To survive, it must be "effective" in the sense of achieving organization purpose and "efficient" in the sense of satisfying individual motives. The executive must preside over and adapt to each other the processes which relate the cooperative system of its environment and which provide satisfaction to individuals.

The initial concept of cooperation leads to the definition of organization as a "system of consciously coordinated activities or forces of two or more persons." Essential to the *survival* of organization is the willingness to cooperate, the ability to communicate the existence and acceptance of purpose. The executive functions are thus to provide a system of communication, to maintain the willingness to cooperate, and to ensure the continuing integrity of organization purpose.

Some time ago, I read a book by Dr. Marshall Goldberg called *The Anatomy Lesson.* In the following passage, the author makes clear the systemic nature of the human body and of the holistic medical knowledge necessary to understand it:

> A young doctor must not only be familiar with his tools but also with the disease process he's treating. And for that the diagnosis is paramount. *I have scant respect for the kind of practitioner who treats a patient's symptoms piece-meal, without ever considering him as a whole person,* one who harbors a disease either of the mind or of the body and capable of affecting both. And in order for you to make correct diagnosis you must apply certain basic principles. If your patient complains of right upper quadrant abdominal pain, you must consider the structures put there by nature which might possibly give rise to such discomfort. Perhaps it's a gallstone or a peptic ulcer; the pathology might lie in the kidney or ascending colon. *Whatever the case, it's your working knowledge of anatomy that's of primary use to you and for that reason we make amply sure you know it.*

In our case, be certain you know the "anatomy" of a nonprofit and of your organization in particular.

Finally, John W. Gardner, in his book *Self-Renewal: The Individual and the Innovative Society,* also discusses systems:

> Every individual, organization or society must mature, but much depends on how this maturing takes place. A society whose maturing consists simply of acquiring more firmly established ways of doing things is headed for the graveyard—even if it learns to do these things with greater and greater skill. *In the ever-renewing society what matures is a system or framework within which continuous innovation, renewal and rebirth can occur.*
>
> A modern view of the processes of growth, decay and renewal must give due emphasis to both continuity and change in human institutions.
>
> Renewal is not just innovation and change. It is also the process of bringing the results of change into line with our purposes. When our

forbears invented the motor car, they had to devise rules of the road. Both are phases of renewal. When urban expansion threatens chaos, we must revise our conceptions of city planning and metropolitan government.

Boards and staff must take a holistic view of their organizations. They must understand not only the individual components of the organization, but also how these components interrelate.

10

Board Policy
What It Is, How It Is Made

Even after years of working with boards, I have yet to hear anyone define "policy" adequately. Policy is generally understood, but is not defined in such a way as to enable boards to say with certainty, "This is a policy, and this is not."

Some publications have lists of items that could be labeled as either board or staff decisions—for example, whether to paint a room (and the color of the paint), whether to hire staff, whether to spend nonbudgeted funds, whether to approve the annual report, and how to set membership standards. A complete list would, of course, cover a number of pages.

I believe there are two guiding principles when thinking about policy. The first is that boards generally decide *what* to do, not *how* to do it. The second principle invokes Peter F. Drucker's effectiveness and efficiency designation: boards tend to make the effective decisions, leaving efficiency to staff. Using Drucker's concept, effectiveness is the "what"; efficiency is the "how." Even this is too general a formulation against which to test a definitive description of what constitutes "policy." The only way to adequately define policy is to put policy in the context of a framework. One framework

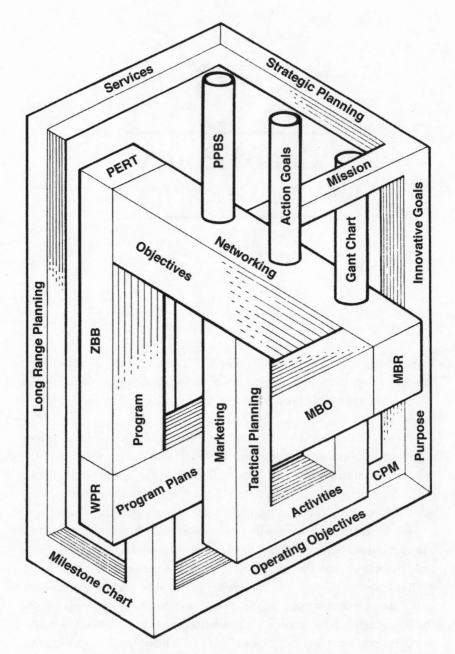

Figure 10-1. Impossible planning

that seems to fit this need is that of "planning." There is, however, little general agreement as to what a planning framework is. There is a profusion of terminology and systems, as illustrated in Figure 10–1.

Hierarchy of Planning

The planning system chosen by an organization provides a common language, how its members talk to each other. Most organizations eventually arrive at what I call a hierarchy of planning.

This quote from Rudyard Kipling helps explain the hierarchy of planning:

> "I keep six honest serving men
> (They taught me all I knew)

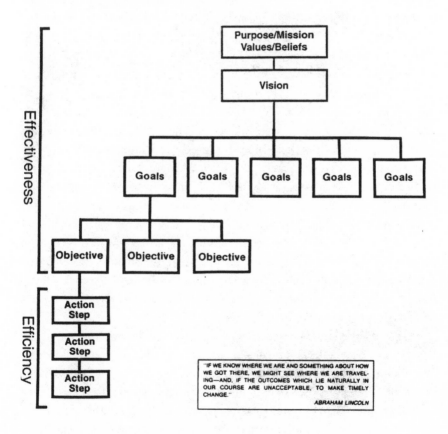

Figure 10–2. Hierarchy of planning

Their names are What and Why and When
and How, and Where and Who."

This fits very nicely with the hierarchy of planning:

- Why—External and Internal Data
  Purpose/Mission
- What—Values/Beliefs
  Goals and Objectives
- How—Programs and Action Steps
  When, Where, and Who are part "How"

Purpose or Mission

Mission is a broad statement of purpose or organizational ends to be achieved. It explains why an organization exists in the first place and is the final test for everything an organization does. It is generally the why and what of the organization.

The purpose *does not* encompass "how" the organization intends to implement its mission; rather, it provides the *direction* for an organization and the *justification* for *all its work*. It serves as a compass in turbulent times.

All missions should be supportable, believable, and desirable. They are usually achievable, though this might take years. An organization's mission statement should be fairly brief, certainly no more than a couple of paragraphs in length. The mission should be all-encompassing: though brief, it should lay out the key purpose of the organization. Simply stating "to serve people" is not enough. Missions commit us to economic efficiency; especially as a not-for-profit organization, we should make a commitment to economic efficiency and effectiveness. The geographic market served by the organization should be included in the mission statement. Are we a local, statewide, regional, national, or international organization? Who are our clients? Why do we serve them?

Although an organization may want to review its mission statement annually, we should be careful about making any major changes. The mission statement should be able to withstand a four- or five-year period without major changes. Of course, if an opportunity presents itself or if some major event occurs, the statement may need to be changed; this step, however, should occur only after very thorough discussion and analysis.

A mission statement should serve as an anchoring device. As well, it ought to tell how the organization is different from other organizations. This is where modeling aspects of the planning process come into play. With what organizations do we wish to be compared? Do we wish to be viewed as a leader or as a follower? How are we different from organizations that have similar purposes?

With so much importance riding on a mission statement, it should go without saying that it must be understandable. Unfortunately, some mission statements are written in such convoluted English and are so full of buzz words and acronyms that they are virtually impossible to understand. Remember that the mission statement is a key part of the strategic planning process. It should be written to express, not to impress.

Values/Beliefs

While the mission statement guides the work of the organization, values or belief statements guide the behavior of the individuals who work for the organization. This statement provides the ethical framework for the organization.

Vision

Once an organization is certain of its purpose or mission, values and beliefs, it can begin to create a vision of the future. Our vision will describe a community that is both different and better because of our work. Imagination is the operative word. A Scottish philosopher, Dugald Stewart, had this to say about imagination:

> The faculty of imagination is the great spring of human activity, and the principal source of human improvement. As it delights in presenting to the mind scenes and characters more perfect than those which we are acquainted with, it prevents us from ever being completely satisfied with our present condition, or with our past attainments, and engages us continually in the pursuit of some untried enjoyment, or of some ideal excellence. Destroy this faculty, and the condition of man will become as stationary as that of the brutes.

Goals

Goals are specific outcomes that provide the definitive direction and planning framework. They are a base for looking into the future, constructing the organization's vision. They are the basis for strategic planning. They are quantifiable over a period of time, usually two to five years.

Objectives

Objectives flow from the confluence of goals and current issues: they are specific outcomes required to achieve a given goal. They are the key to planning implementation. Objectives provide the basis for writing budgets. We can recognize at least two types of objectives:

- Process: These last the entire fiscal period.
- Event: These occur at a specific time, then are concluded.

"The club will offer a full schedule of sport teams for boys and girls, ages 9–16" is an example of a process objective. "The annual meeting will be held on February 10" is an example of an event objective.

Action Steps

These are the steps or tasks to be taken to achieve objectives. Using Kipling's words, action steps are the "how" of planning; they also include when and where specific actions are to be taken and who is responsible for carrying them out.

Planning and the Work to Be Done

To lay the foundation for defining policy, we must add the concept of the hierarchy of planning to the Work to Be Done model we developed in earlier chapters, illustrated in Figure 10–3.

Let's call the combination "Work to Be Done II," as illustrated in Figure 10–4.

So, what is policy? From my point of view, board policy or board decisions are purpose or mission, values or beliefs, vision, goals, and objectives. Programs and action steps are part of policy implementation and, as such, they are staff decisions. Although our example in Figure 10–4 shows

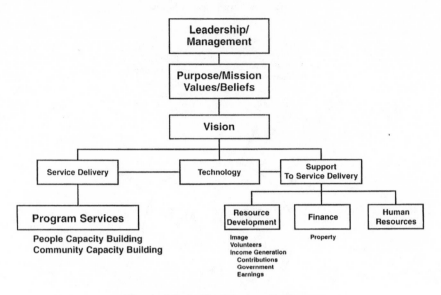

Figure 10-3. The Work to Be Done

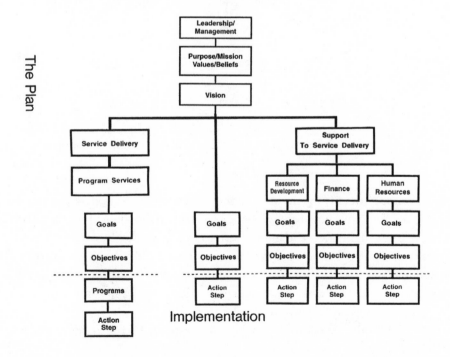

Figure 10-4. The Work to Be Done II

Figure 10-5. The Work to Be Done II as a source of information

the framework only for the areas of service delivery and support to service delivery, one could easily construct a similar chart for the areas of resource development, finance, and human resources or any other "work" of the organization. As always, each organization must build its own Work to Be Done framework. Once an organization has developed its Work to Be Done, it should be written out, enlarged, and placed in a prominent position at every board, committee, and staff meeting.

Finally, the "Work to Be Done II" is the source of crucial information, as illustrated by Figure 10-5.

The Board Policy Process:
Development, Decision, Implementation, Evaluation

All too often, the policy determination process of voluntary boards of directors can be summed up in words like those of one would-be staff executive: "My board doesn't make policy—I do. They don't know enough to really be able to help me in my job. What they do, in effect, is simply ratify my policy." Melvin E. Sims, president of FS Services, Inc., does better in his speech entitled "Management-Board Relations, A Board President's View":

> Regardless of the chief executive officer's attitude concerning the importance of, or the competency of, the board of directors, it is prudent to remember that the board has the legal authority to impose its will. The manager who views his board as an unnecessary nuisance flirts with disaster, both for his own future career and for the future of the cooperative. Sooner or later, a director will read the articles of incorporation and the bylaws and fully comprehend the powers vested in the board.

Although this speech was delivered to a group of businessmen, the concept embodied in it reflects the reality of the situation in voluntary organizations. Further on, Mr. Sims made some critically important comments with respect to policy considerations:

> Although it does not appear in the job description of many chief executive officers, he has a significant responsibility in the area of training and development of the board of directors. He spends more time with the board, as a group, than any other person and has a unique opportunity to teach by supervising actual experiences. If a member of the board gets into operating activities, the manager should make him aware of the division of responsibility if the chairperson fails to do so. Obviously, the manager must know the difference between operating and policy questions. Generally speaking, if it is a matter of what is to be done or where the cooperative is to go, it probably lies in the policy area. If, on the other hand, it is a question of how the work is to be done or who is to do it, it probably lies in the operating area and should be a decision of the manager.
>
> The manager should have an active part in policy development. He is close to the problems and has staff available to assist in doing research. Broad policy determination, however, is clearly a policy decision to be made by the board. For instance, the basic objective of the cooperative is a fundamental decision for the board to make.
>
> I feel strongly that the manager should present his recommendation in

writing. Each recommendation should be presented in a brief and concise statement following a commentary which enumerates the alternatives and the advantages and disadvantages of the proposition. A written statement is generally more carefully researched, more clearly stated, and more easily understood—and it becomes a matter of record. A sensitive manager, who really knows his board, should be able to generally predict how every director will react to a given recommendation. He should be able to anticipate almost every question and have an accurate, complete answer—either in the commentary or available during the discussion period.

There are some who differ with me, but I believe that most recommendations, if not all, should be approved by the board if the manager recommends them. If a manager brings a large number of recommendations to the board which are turned down, the organization probably needs a new manager. As a director, I want recommendations to be brought to me which are thoroughly researched, carefully analyzed, and can be approved with comfort and conviction.

Directors should raise questions and express reservations, if there are any. Directors may even try to talk the manager out of an idea, but if he persists, I am inclined to allow him to try his plan, unless it carries the risk of seriously damaging or destroying the cooperative. Even though the board is ultimately charged with managing the affairs of the cooperative, they must delegate the responsibility and authority to a full time professional manager. My philosophy is to employ a manager, give him advice, and counsel but let him manage, judge his performance, and replace him if the results are not satisfactory.

I offer this long quote because it contains critical concepts for the board-staff and board-chief staff officer relationships. See if you can find the following concepts in the text of Mr. Sims's comments and apply them to your own situation:

- CSO role in board training and development
- Board incursion into staff operations
- Differences between policy and implementation
- CSO and staff roles in policy development
- Presentation of CSO and staff recommendations
- Board approval of staff recommendations
- Board inquiry
- Delegation of authority
- Philosophy of board relationship to CSO

Perhaps the most important things to emphasize are that policy definition and formulation are the foundations for effective and efficient board/

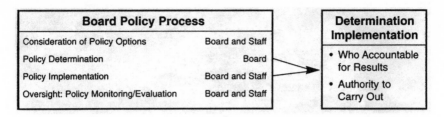

Figure 10-6. Board policy process

staff relations and that in formulating policy, directors must act legally and ethically. Of course, a board of directors can delegate, but it cannot abdicate its accountability for the results of that delegation.

Three of the four steps listed in Figure 10-6 are achieved by the board and staff working together. Only in policy determination does the board act alone. Note particularly that at the implementation step, both board and staff are involved: the board must accept responsibility for the results of the policies it has promulgated.

Board members are responsible for what they delegate. The board may delegate implementation of a policy to the executive. The executive, in turn, may delegate to the assistant executive director. The assistant executive director may then delegate to the program supervisor. The program supervisor may delegate further to the social worker. But in the end, the board of directors is responsible for what the social worker does. It has delegated the authority to the executive director to hire the social worker and will, no doubt, hold the executive responsible for what the social worker does, but ultimate responsibility still resides with the board.

It is most important to note that policy determination actually has three parts:

1. The decision to adopt a particular policy.
2. The parties accountable for the results of the policy.
3. The parties authorized to carry it out.

Many boards stop at the first point. Boards sometimes decide they will do something, then blame the executive if it doesn't happen. Fund-raising is a good example. The board might agree to raise $100,000 and then blame the executive if the goal is not reached. The board must make the path of accountability clear. Remember, the board cannot avoid the second part of

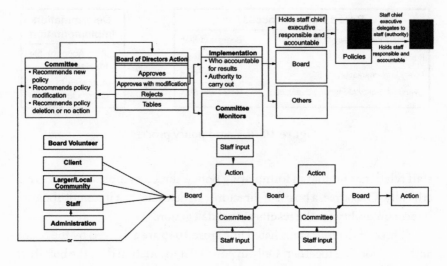

Figure 10-7. Policy formulation

policy determination. Again, the board of directors is responsible for all that happens within its organization. *Boards may delegate—they may not abdicate.*

So, where does policy come from? It can come from anybody. Hopefully, most of the recommendations will come to the board from or through a committee. Realistically, ninety percent of all recommendations will come from the staff assigned to the committee after thorough discussion. The recommendation then moves as illustrated in Figure 10-7.

Remember, the committee is responsible for monitoring the results of its recommendation if the board approves. Although the board can delegate to others aside from the staff chief executive, the executive must keep track of all that affects his or her organization. The board of directors must have some mechanism to allow clients and the community to contribute ideas and expertise. Board volunteers have direct access to policy determination; interested others have no such access unless the board creates a point of entry in the deliberative process.

Suppose an issue of a policy nature comes to the board, an issue which the staff has neither seen nor heard of. What happens? Board meetings are not staff meetings; staff have no role except to respond when asked. However, if the board does decide to open the issue to discussion, the staff has the right to offer input—even to the extent of requesting the issue be tabled until staff has had an opportunity to review it. If the board refers the issue to a committee, then any staff input should go through that committee. When the issue returns to the board for a decision, staff has no further input.

One important example of staff's approach to the board is the grievance procedure. It is important that the board make clear what issues the staff may bring before the board. If the board allows too much staff input about management, it will undercut the ability of the executive to manage. The grievance procedure should confine itself to issues in the human resources Work to Be Done.

Some examples of legitimate grievances are:

- Being hired for a position and given a salary outside the range and level stipulated in the personnel policies;
- Being denied fringe benefits guaranteed in the personnel policies;
- Being denied time off (vacations, absences, and so on) guaranteed in the personnel policies;
- Performance evaluation conducted in violation of the personnel policies;
- Being hired for a position and finding that the actual work does not correspond to the job description presented at the interview.

In any organization, there is always the problem of distinguishing between democracy and discipline. Democracy extends to the point of decision—all parties are involved in the discussion and, in specific cases, the vote. Once a decision is made, however, discipline must take over. Both staff and board members are bound by the decision—whether or not they voted for it.

Before closing this chapter, the issues of power and manipulation require examination. Inherent to the word "manipulate" is the notion of using something with skill. Unfortunately, negative connotations also arise, such as juggling or falsification. Staff has the responsibility to assist its board volunteers in the pursuit of the lawful purposes, goals, and objectives of the organization. This is not manipulation in its darker connotation; it is positive motivation.

Manipulation in its negative sense may manifest itself in the improper exercise of the staff's power. Staff, especially in education, has always been concerned with power—or, rather, its lack of it. The argument is that if boards have the power to set and dictate policy, then staff is essentially powerless to influence the decision-making process. This contention overlooks the greater, more subtle power of persuasion. Persuasion is a product of the power of knowledge. By virtue of working full time, the staff executive has

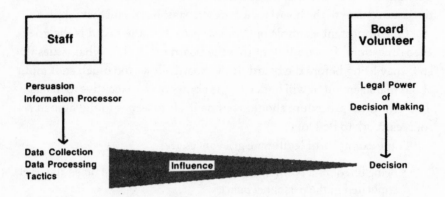

Figure 10-8. Power and control of information

more knowledge about the operational aspects of the particular organization and its requirements than has the board volunteer. Dr. H. Durward Hofler deals with this issue very well in his paper, "Voluntary Organizations":

> Knowledge is a form of power and control; by implication, lack of knowledge means a loss of power and control. Thus, for example, withholding and/or providing misleading information is not an uncommon means of controlling another person's behavior against what would be his will were he given fuller, more accurate information.

Further on, Dr. Hofler contends that "real decision-making power often is in the hands of information processors instead of in the hands of those who formally make decisions." In this context, the information processor is the staff member and the decision-maker is the board member.

While this process is natural—and even advantageous where trust exists—as the staff begins to withhold or process information in order to influence decisions of board volunteers, it becomes truly manipulative in the sinister sense. There is no quicker way for the trust between board volunteer and staff to be destroyed than through the processing of information by the staff in order to influence board decisions. It sets a terrible trap into which it is easy to fall and must be continuously guarded against. Florence Nightingale provides an interesting quote on this topic. She apparently said this after the reality of working with a group of volunteers collided with her ideals:

Staff	Board Volunteers		
FACTS	**MR. SMITH**	**MR. BROWN**	**MR. JONES**
A	A	B	A
B	B	C	B
C	C	D	C
D	F	E	D
E			F
F			

Figure 10-9. Manipulation of information

When I entered "into service" here, I determined that, happen what would, I never would intrigue among the committee. Now I perceive that I do all my business by intrigue. I propose in private, to A, B, or C the resolution I think A, B, or C most capable of carrying in committee, and then leave it to them, and I always win.

This point is further illustrated by Figure 10-9. Staff has facts A through F. Staff is selective as to who gets the facts to influence a decision. It may work once, even twice; but once it is found out, trust will surely evaporate.

Section IV

How to Assemble a Board

11

Selecting and Recruiting Board Members

Recall that earlier I suggested the board of directors, in addition to being a system in and of itself, is also part of a larger system called the nonprofit organization. No component of either system can function effectively without the effective functioning of the whole system. Keep this point in mind as you read this chapter.

The board membership process includes attracting board volunteers, determining how they are to be treated, and, when necessary, deciding how to separate them when they are not productive. If the process is done well, the motivation of board volunteers is considerably enhanced.

The crucial point in the board membership process arrives when the candidate is approached with "We need you!" The candidate usually responds: "What for?" *What for?!* In the answer to this question lies the key to recruiting a board member, to an effective board, and, in the long term, to a successful voluntary organization.

Consider the following two scenarios. Each illustrates a very narrow and self-destructive view of the role of the voluntary board member.

Scenario One

Scene:	A board meeting of a voluntary organization. During the meeting Joe Goodfriend waves his hand for the recognition of the board chairperson, Herman Easygoing.
Herman:	Before we go on to the next item of business, let's see what Joe has on his mind.
Joe:	Thanks, Herman. I've got with me Stanley Opportunist. Stan is a neighbor of mine—we've known each other for years. Last Sunday we were talking over cocktails and dinner. I happened to mention I was a member of this outstanding board and told him about all the important people who belong to it. He thought it sounded interesting and wondered if he could join. I thought it was a great idea and brought Stan with me today. He's a good man, and our board could use him. I recommend him for membership. Let's vote on him.
Herman:	Joe, a friend of yours is a friend of ours. All in favor of Stanley Opportunist for board membership say "aye." Opposed? Carried unanimously. Welcome to our board, Mr. Opportunist. Now, the next item of business.

This scenario is all too frequent. Boards are always looking for new blood. This board, however, lacks any process for presenting new prospective members. The sole criterion in voting on the candidate was his being a friend of Joe. Election to a board is official board business; the candidate should *not* be present during deliberations or voting. Any meaningful discussion of the candidate's qualifications will be stifled in the candidate's presence.

Scenario Two

Scene:	The office of George Munch, president of Ace Corporation. Mr. Munch is a member of the board of directors of the Hometown Organization and has been given the assignment of recruiting Lawrence S. Powerful, president of Powderpuff Industries. Mr. Munch's secretary has just reached Mr. Powerful by telephone.
Mr. Munch:	Hi, Larry—quite a party you had last night! Thanks for the invitation. I meant to ask you, did you ever close that deal for Boodeen Company? . . . Fell through, huh? Too bad. Say,

Larry, are you and Sally going to be able to join Viv and me at the Country Club dance next month? . . . Great! It's going to be a first-class affair. What did you decide about that boat? Are you going to get the six or eight sleeping capacity? . . . Sounds good. You should enjoy it. Sure, we'd like to cruise down to Florida. Let's clear our calendars and do it . . . Oh, you have a staff meeting in a few minutes. Look, this will only take a minute. You know I'm on the board of the Hometown Organization—would you care to join our board? . . . No, it doesn't take a lot of time. Just one meeting a month and none during the summer . . . No, there isn't much to do. Having your name associated with us will be a great help . . . What does the Hometown Organization do? Our big job is keeping the kids off the street—you know, keep them under close supervision and they won't be running around breaking windows and stealing . . . Good, I'll submit your name . . . Yes, I know you'll be too busy to come to any meetings for the next three or four months . . . Glad to have you aboard, Larry. See you tomorrow afternoon for a round of golf at the Club. Bye.

The four most important decisions of the board of directors, in order of priority, are:

- Performance evaluation of the CSO
- Selection of the CSO
- Selection of the CBO
- Selection of new board members

The selection and recruitment of new board members is a very serious decision. The health and vitality of a nonprofit organization depend upon a committed, involved, and energized board of directors.

The image, selection, and recruitment phases will clarify what is expected of the candidate, and do much to establish the climate in which he or she will work. The orientation, continuing education, and recognition phases will determine the individual's effectiveness as a board volunteer.

1. *Image* is what the public thinks of the organization. A poor community image will make it virtually impossible to recruit key leadership.

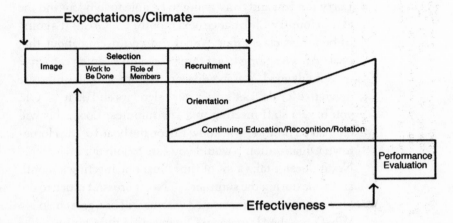

Figure 11–1. Board membership process

2. *Selection* means careful scrutiny of candidates against agreed-upon criteria.
3. *Recruitment* means putting together the best plan and personnel to per-suade the candidate to serve on the board.
4. Recruitment is the introduction to *orientation;* where recruitment ends, orientation begins. In the recruitment phase, the board volunteer is given an overview of the organization. The orientation phase, on the other hand, is more in-depth. While the recruitment phase is con-cerned primarily with what the organization does, the orientation phase is concerned with *how* the organization functions.
5. Recruitment and orientation also include *continuing education.* After orientation is over, education continues for as long as the board volun-teer remains. The education of a board volunteer includes both prepa-ration for, and assistance in, executing his or her role.
6. *Recognition.* Saying thanks for jobs well done is essential.
7. *Rotation* of board volunteers to different positions and committees is also important.
8. *Performance evaluations* determine how well a board volunteer has per-formed in his or her role and are important to deciding whether the member is renominated or dropped.

The components of the board membership process are the responsi-bility of several different committees. These responsibilities and the corre-sponding committees are listed here:

Image:	Image Committee
Selection:	Board Membership Subcommittee
Recruitment:	Board Membership Subcommittee
Orientation:	Board of Directors
Election:	Board of Directors
Continuing Education:	Board Membership Subcommittee
Rotation:	Board Membership Subcommittee
Performance/Evaluation:	Board of Directors

The board membership subcommittee of the resource development committee is usually a standing subcommittee, as its activities are conducted year-round. Because the nominations take place only once a year, a separate ad hoc nominating committee should be formed to perform the following functions:

I. Evaluation of board members up for re-election
    A. Unqualified renomination of all-around good board members
    B. Programmed renomination for those members of evident potential, but who haven't found the key to greater involvement
    C. Programmed separation for those board members best asked to leave the board
II. The nomination of officers

The basic reason for separating the nominating function from the board membership function is that such a system of checks and balances inhibits the growth of cliques and tends to keep the evaluation process unbiased. *Those who recruit should not also evaluate.*

A board of directors is best divided into thirds, so that only the term of one third of all board volunteers expires annually. New board volunteers should be elected to a full three-year term or to complete the term of a member who has left the board prematurely.

In a nominating committee meeting, committee members receive, for each board member up for nomination, a folder containing such data as are necessary to evaluate that board member. Information that may be helpful includes records of the candidate's service on the boards of other nonprofit organizations. Although board experience is a positive factor, be cautious if the candidate already serves on four or more nonprofit boards. The broader the participation, the less time the candidate has for each board. Service on corporate boards of directors is also a useful indicator of the qualifications of a prospective board member, as is his or her reputation at any business or organization in which the candidate serves. Other factors for consideration are listed later in this chapter.

Nominating committee members should be independent of any power cliques on the board. An elected nominating committee probably has a better chance than an appointed one in escaping such an influence. Members should also be sufficiently secure in their own professions, businesses, and communities to objectively evaluate candidates. Of course, the committee members should also be well acquainted with the organization's goals and objectives and the resulting leadership needs. They should also be well enough acquainted with the role requirements of a board volunteer to make sound judgments on the qualifications of candidates.

Committee members should have sufficient stature in the community to enable them to make any contacts necessary to recruiting new volunteers. If they have already arrived socially or are well-established in their businesses, they will be less likely, when selecting people, to substitute personal needs for the needs of the organization. In the case of urban volunteer organizations, it is important to represent the community sector on both committees. Too many organizations have little representation from the constituencies they serve. Organizations serving local communities may be viewed as aloof or as lacking knowledge and perspective if community members are not included on the board. Lack of representation from within a constituency deprives the board of useful information and may create a public relations nightmare.

It is best if those serving on the membership committee have sufficient knowledge of the community to actually *represent* it. Remember that although a prospective member may belong to a particular racial, ethnic, social, or business group, it does not automatically follow that he or she represents that group. There is a difference between real and apparent power; real power in a community is, many times, completely anonymous. I recall one organization that had what appeared to be excellent community representation on its board of directors. I found three ministers, two block club presidents, two teachers, and one principal on this board. Yet the organization did not have a positive image, even though its services were adequate. In talking with members of the community, I found that these individuals were not trusted, even though they were of the same race as most of the organization's constituency. These people were generally viewed as publicity seekers, more interested in their own connections than in the community. This board made the mistake of recruiting the most visible, not the most influential.

It constantly amazes me how much evasion and downright dishonesty take place at the recruitment interview when the candidate asks, "Why choose me for membership?" Those who want a candidate for his money will deny it. If the candidate is expected to raise money, this is often revealed only after he or she agrees to join. The time commitment for membership is often described as "just a few meetings." Those who want only the candidate's name will emphasize a function he can serve.

Why all this deceit? Candor will better serve both the candidate and the organization. Are we really afraid to tell people what we do, that it takes *work* to be a good board member? Or are the recruiters as ignorant of the truth as is the candidate? Are staff executives afraid to be frank? Are they afraid of building strong boards? Recruiting must be, above all, *honest*.

I once worked with the chairperson of a board membership committee who felt it was not appropriate to reveal all the relevant organizational information to board candidates. "If we told them everything, they probably wouldn't join. Let them find out once they are on the board" was the general attitude. The areas in which information was withheld included fundraising, attendance at board meetings, and the time commitment involved in board service. Needless to say, the attrition rate of board members recruited in this way was nearly one hundred percent. This committee chairperson lasted only nine months in the position, but did a lot of damage in that time.

Staff and other board volunteers must not make value judgments about a candidate's reasons for joining. But why do people join boards? If today's boards are going to be as diverse as they need to be, we have to know a bit about why a volunteer joins and what his or her needs are. These concepts apply to all board volunteers, regardless of socioeconomic considerations.

People join boards to satisfy needs. The eight items listed in Figure 11–2 are meant to be representative, not exhaustive. We simply need to recognize that an individual's willingness to accept board service rests, in large measure, on his on her reasons for joining the board in the first place. Increased response to board service demands is brought about through a board volunteer's *involvement* (see left side of chart).

On the left side of Figure 11–3 are three reasons for joining a board which share a common characteristic: they tend to be *growth-facilitating*. In

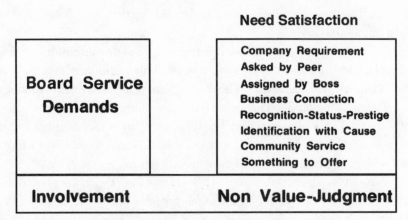

Figure 11-2. Need satisfaction and involvement

other words, from the outset, there exists a climate conducive to increased involvement and productivity.

The right side of the chart lists five other reasons for joining a board, which we will characterize as *static*. Those who join for any of these reasons tend to remain at the same level of minimal involvement. The secret of increased commitment is the fostering of personal growth. This should begin with recruitment and orientation and continue throughout a person's board service.

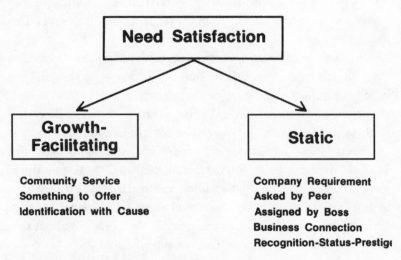

Figure 11-3. Growth facilitation versus stasis

Higher Degree of Goal Integration
Results in better organizational functioning, greater satisfaction of individual's organizational role

Figure 11-4. Goal integration

Some organizational theory suggests that the greater the goal integration within an organization, the greater the satisfaction of its members and the smoother its operation. Look at Figure 11-4. Increased communication is the key to increasing goal integration.

Of course, goal integration is never total, nor should we expect it to be. Some degree of goal integration, however, is necessary for success. A board never fully matures until it can identify with the organization's cause or purpose. It is their *commitment* which causes board volunteers to move outside themselves to what Lord Moulton called "obedience to the unenforceable."

Phases of the Board Membership Process

Image

A candidate for board membership judges the organization even before recruitment interviews ever begin. He or she will already have some notion of the organization from radio, television, comments from his or her peers, subordinates, and superiors, newspapers, magazines, and the organization's literature. Based on a particular circumstance or series of circumstances, his or her notions may range anywhere from a vague impression to a thoroughly hardened opinion. The image may be positive (the organization is well-known and respected); neutral (not much is known about the organization or it is entirely unknown); or even negative (the organization has a poor public image as a result of unfavorable incidents or inadequate facilities, staff, programs, and support). Recruitment is simplified by a positive image. When the organization's image is neutral, considerable persuasion must be brought to bear. Recruitment is practically impossible when a negative image exists.

Image is a composite of public relations and publicity. Publicity is the program the organization generates to create a favorable impression in the community, such as radio and television spots, billboards, posters, newspaper and magazine articles, and community involvement. Public relations refers to what the public thinks about the organization after the public comes in contact with a piece of publicity. Board volunteers, staff, and clients are all public relations agents. A million dollars in publicity can be lost by one poorly handled phone call or misused contribution.

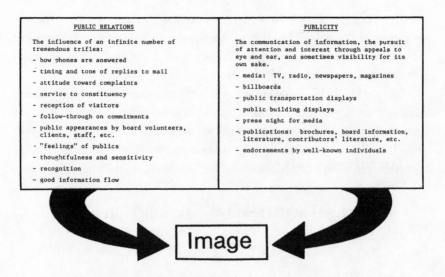

Figure 11–5. Public relations, publicity, and image

Selection

Too often, the first step in the board membership process is to ask, "Whom do we want?" The usual result is a list of names annotated with vague comments like, "He or she will do a lot for us!" What exactly that person can do is rarely defined. It is better to ask *why* a particular person would be a desirable board member. Unless there are well-defined criteria for the work to be accomplished by the board of directors, there is no way to intelligently recruit an individual. Know exactly the work to be done, and think of the individual candidate within this framework. Know also the specific function that recruit will fulfill once on the board.

There are two major considerations in candidate selection, and many secondary ones. Here's an outline.

I. Personal Considerations
   A. Does he or she have stature in the community?
   B. Does he or she have interest in the organization?
   C. Does he or she have leadership potential?
   D. Does he or she have communication skills?
   E. Is he or she available?
   F. Is he or she affluent or influential?
   G. What are his or her spheres of influence?
   H. Does he or she have integrity?
   I. Is the candidate successful in his or her own field?
II. Knowledge and Skills

Knowledge and skills must be matched to the requirements of the board. Figures 11-6 and 11-7 are forms useful in setting criteria for knowledge and skills required for board membership. The criteria listed across the top are only an example of what can be developed by an organization to match their board requirements. The process for preparation of this form is as follows:

1. The board of directors commissions the resource development committee to recommend a format. The work is done by the board membership subcommittee.
2. The board membership subcommittee reports to the board with a suggested format.
3. Once the format is approved, the committee places the names of the board volunteers down the left side and makes check marks in the appropriate boxes. By adding up the check marks at the bottom of the columns, requirements for new volunteers should be clear. Once this

Figure 11-6

NEWPORT ORGANIZATION	BOARD COMPOSITION ANALYSIS		
SANCTION	Medical		
	Small Businesses		
	Local Media		
	Churches		
	Corporate		
	Political		
	Education		
	Law Enforcement		
	Neighborhood		
RACE OR ETHNIC	Asian American		
	Native American		
	African American		
	Hispanic		
	(Relevant to community)		
SEX	Female		
	Male		
AGE	Over 65		
	51 – 65		
	22 – 50		
	17 – 21		
	YEARS ON BOARD		
		BOARD MEMBER	

Figure 11–6. Knowledge and skills assessment—1

Figure 11-7

POLICY DETERMINATION	PERSONNEL	Personnel Policy	
		Fringe Benefits	
		Performance Appraisal	
		Wage & Salary Admin.	
	RESOURCE DEV.	Image	
		Identify Prospects for Board Membership	
		Annual Giving	
		Planned Giving	
		Capital Giving	
	FINANCE	Property Management	
		Budgeting/Fiscal Control	
	PROGRAMS	Vocational	
		Arts	
		Group Work	
		Counseling	
		Health and PE	
		Education	
RESOURCE DEVELOPMENT		Access to Material contributions	
		Access to contributed services	
		Direct Mail	
		Access to Foundation	
		Access to individuals with money	
		Access to corporations	
		Personal wealth	

Figure 11–7. Knowledge and skills assessment—2

form is shared with the board, it is possible for the board to suggest candidates based on these criteria.

Following are additional considerations:

Politics	Education	Health
Republican	A.B.	Good
Democrat	M.S.	Poor
Independent	Doctorate	
Liberal	Professional	
Conservative	None	

Wealth (net worth)	Religion
$1,000,000 plus	Roman Catholic
$500,000 to $1,000,000	Jewish
$250,000 to $500,000	Protestant (all denominations)
$100,000 to $250,000	Other
Under $100,000	

Annual income	
$1,000,000	$25,000 to $49,000
$500,000 to $1,000,000	$10,000 to $24,000
$100,000 to $500,000	Under $10,000
$50,000 to $99,000	Unknown

Figure 11–8 is a suggested format for a candidate form to be filled out by present board volunteers and submitted to the board membership subcommittee.

Recruitment

After a candidate has been selected, the next phase of the board membership process is recruitment. The first step is to put together a recruitment plan based on knowledge of the candidate and to select the most effective people to ask the candidate to undertake board service. People often agree to join boards based on who invites them. This is a critical element in developing a recruitment plan. Remember that the recruitment phase focuses more on *what* the organization does, while orientation concerns *how* the organization does it.

NEWPORT ORGANIZATION

CANDIDATE FOR BOARD MEMBERSHIP

(Prepared by the Sponsoring Member of the Board of Directors)

Name: _____

Address (Business): _____ Tel. _____

           (Home): _____ Tel. _____

Occupation & Position: _____

Education and/or Training: _____

_____

Honors: _____

Organizations: _____

_____

Charitable Activities in which he/she is *actively* engaged: _____

_____

_____

What are his/her current interests in the Newport Organization? ___

_____

_____

What activities would particularly interest him/her? _____

_____

_____

Willing to engage in fund raising? _____

Your personal recommendation: _____

_____

_____

                                Sponsor: _____

                                Date: _____

Figure 11-8. Sample board candidate form

NEWPORT ORGANIZATION

STAFF EXECUTIVE'S CHECKLIST FOR NEW BOARD VOLUNTEERS

NAME _____ ACCEPTED ON _____

	CHECKLIST		COMPLETED
1.	Personal History File Folder Prepared		
2.	Board of Directors Individual Contribution Record prepared (see page 6 of the Voluntary Management Press publication, *Nominating Committee Manual of Operation*)		
3.	Board Volunteer Personal Data	Mailed	
		Received	
		Follow Up	
4.	Photograph received		
5.	Letter of Welcome from executive director		
6.	Letter of Welcome from Chairperson of the Board with copy to Executive Director		
7.	Letter of Welcome from Chairperson of Committee with copies to chairperson of Board and Executive Director		
8.	Letter from Campaign Chairperson		
9.	Visit from Campaign Team Captain		
10.	Orientation Session Set Up		
11.	Metro News Release Sent		
12.	Local News Release Sent		
13.	Company House Organ Release		

Figure 11–9. Staff executive checklist for new board volunteers

When meeting a candidate, members of the recruiting board should discuss the following:

I. Estimating Time Requirements of Board Membership
    A. Active Board Participation—three to six hours monthly. This includes:
        1. Board meetings
        2. Committee meetings
        3. Fund-raising
        4. Meetings with staff
        5. Telephone calls. This varies according to the time of year (summers are light) and the activities scheduled (fund-raising is heavy from October to April).

NEWPORT ORGANIZATION

Orientation for _____ SALLY E. JONES _____ Date _____

Committee Assignment _____ PERSONNEL

ITEM	TIME	PLACE	STAFF/BD.	PICK UP TIME & PLACE
1. Site visit	2 hrs.	Unit I & II	Exec. Dir.	Exec. pick up at SEJ's Off. 10 a.m. 10/12
2. Administration —Structure—Bd. & Staff —Role & Function of Bd. & Staff. —Planning Program	1 hr.	SEJ's Off.	Board Chr. & Exec. Dir.	At SEJ's Off. 2 p.m. 10/14
3. Program Services	1 hr.	Adm. Off.	Pro. Dir. & Chr. of P.S. Comm.	Will come at Noon 10/18
4. Resource Development —Support —Image —Volunteers	1 hr.	Adm. Off.	Dir. of Res. Dev., Chr. of R.D. Comm.	Will come at 10 a.m. 10/20
5. Finance —Budget —Property —Investment	1 hr.	Adm. Off.	Dir. of Finance	Will come at 1 p.m. 10/21
6. Human Resources	3 hrs.	Adm. Off.	Dir. of Human Res.	Will come at 1 p.m. 10/21
TOTAL TIME	9 hrs.			

Figure 11–10. Orientation schedule

B. Leadership Responsibilities—an additional two to four hours monthly. This includes assuming such positions as:
1. Board chairperson
2. Other board positions
3. Committee chairperson
4. Campaign chairperson
5. Campaign vice-chairperson
6. Campaign team captain
7. Representative of board at other organization functions

II. The recruiter then gives the candidate "Your Invitation to Service," or its equivalent. (The kit is presented at the end of the interview.) Two sample covers follow. The staff executive discusses the first three sections with the candidate.
    A. What the organization does—material in "Service" publication, slides, films, or flip charts.
    B. How the organization is organized.
    C. Budget.
III. The board member discusses the function and role of the board volunteer and the function and role of the staff. At this time, the candidate is informed of the specific committee for which he or she is being recruited. Because the work of the board is carried out through committees, it seems appropriate to assign a candidate at the outset. This issue is further discussed under "Rotation." Before a candidate officially assents to having his or her name nominated for election, many organizations are asking candidates to go through orientation. Sometimes a candidate will agree to recruitment, but then change his or her mind after orientation. It is better to have them drop out at the outset rather than become deadwood later.
IV. Follow-up
    A. A letter from the chairperson of the board informing the candidate of his or her election.
    B. A letter of welcome from the staff chief executive.
    C. A letter from the chairperson of his or her selected committee containing the following:
        1. Welcome to the board and to his or her committee
        2. Committee commission
        3. Minutes of the past several committee and board meetings
        4. Request for an appointment to get acquainted and for orientation (followed by a phone call)
        5. A letter of welcome from the campaign chairperson containing the following:
            a. Welcome to the board
            b. Campaign job in current years
            c. Campaign structure
            d. His or her team assignment
        6. A letter from the campaign team-captain containing the following:
            a. Welcome to the board
            b. Request for visit to discuss campaign role
        7. Publicity releases should go to:
            a. Metropolitan media
            b. New board volunteer's home community newspaper

NEWPORT ORGANIZATION

BOARD VOLUNTEER INFORMATION

(CONFIDENTIAL)

NAME: _____ BIRTH DATE: (Day & Month) _____

ADDRESS: _____ TELEPHONE: _____

ZIP CODE: _____ DATE ELECTED TO BOARD: _____

NAME OF SPOUSE: _____ BIRTH DATE: (Day & Month) _____

NUMBER OF CHILDREN: DAUGHTERS _____ SONS _____

EDUCATION: (College attended and type of degree or degrees received)

FRATERNITY MEMBERSHIP:

MEMBERSHIP IN ASSOCIATIONS, SERVICE CLUBS, SOCIAL CLUBS: (include offices held and committees served on)

POLITICAL OFFICES HELD:

CIVIC APPOINTMENTS HELD:

MEMBERSHIP IN OTHER VOLUNTARY ORGANIZATIONS: (Include offices held and committees served on)

REFERRED FOR BOARD MEMBERSHIP BY:

RECRUITED TO THE BOARD BY:

ARE YOU AVAILABLE FOR: TV Shows _____ Radio Programs _____

HOBBIES AND SPECIAL INTERESTS:

For publicity purposes, please send a photograph. If you do not have one, we would like, with your permission, to send a photographer to take one.

Please return to:

Company _____

Address _____

Phone _____

Figure 11–11. Confidential information sheet

    c. New board volunteer's company newsletter

    d. New board volunteer's trade, professional, or other associational newspaper and magazines

  8. A board volunteer's confidential information sheet is sent out. (See Figure 11–11.)

Orientation

The staff chief executive can then conduct orientation. As stated in the previous section, the recruitment phase is designed to give the prospective board volunteer an overview of what the organization does. The orientation phase is designed to give the prospective board volunteer (or new board volunteer) a much broader perspective—*how* the organization does its work.

The objective is to bring the board volunteer to a productive work level as soon as possible. The orientation should be both general—addressing the overall functioning of the organization—and pertinent to the committee structure—a board volunteer should be recruited to a specific committee. One-half to two-thirds of the orientation should be general, and the balance devoted to discussion specific to committee assignment.

General orientation should be conducted by staff and board volunteers in coordination with the executive director or his designate, such as the director of resource development or the associate or assistant executive director.

The orientation should follow the management divisions. A prospective or new board volunteer should receive a three-ring binder, empty except for five dividers or tabs: one each for administration, business, personnel, resource development, and program services. As the recruit moves through orientation, appropriate material can be added to each section. At the end of the orientation process, the new board volunteer has a complete manual of operation. Figure 11–12 is a sample form showing orientation flow and assignments.

Committee orientation should be conducted by the committee chairperson or his or her committee designate and the staff person assigned to the committee. The committee commission, samples of activities of the committee for the previous twelve-month period, and the committee minutes for the previous twelve-month period should all be covered.

NEWPORT ORGANIZATION

CONFERENCE ON BOARDS

"Conceptual Consistency/Operational Diversity"

Date: May 28, 29, 30, 20__
Place: Newport Country Club

1st Day, May 28—Concepts and Framework

10:00 a.m.	*Opening Remarks*
10:15-12:00	*The Board Survey*
12:30 p.m.	*Lunch*
2:00-4:00 p.m.	*The Voluntary Concept*

> *1. Components of Voluntary Organization*
> *2. Role and Function of the Staff*
> *3. Board Structure*
> *4. Role and Function of the Board Volunteer*
> *5. Board Policy Process and Policy Implementation*
> *6. Involvement/Contribution Ratio*
> *7. The Delicate Balance*

4:00-5:00 p.m.	*Board Volunteers as Clients*
5:00-6:00 p.m.	*Diagnosis and Action*
6:30 p.m.	*Supper*

2nd Day, May 29—Nuts and Bolts

9:00-11:00 a.m.	*The Mythology and Methodology of the Staff Role*
10:30 a.m.	*Coffee and Rolls*
11:30-12:00	*The Organization of the Newport Organization*

> *1. The Board of Directors*
> *2. Parallel Organization of Boards of Managers*
> *3. Board/Staff Relationships and Accountability*
> *4. The Bylaws*

12:00 noon	*Lunch*
1:30-3:00 p.m.	*Board and Committee Relationships*

> *1. The Committee Commission*
> *2. Make-up of Board and Committees*
> *3. Ad-Hoc Committees*
> *4. Agenda Building*
> *5. Meetings*
> *6. Minutes*

3:00-3:15 p.m.	*Break*
3:15-5:30 p.m.	*Newport Organization Committee Commissions and Making Them Work*
5:30-6:30 p.m.	*Diagnosis and Action*
7:00 p.m.	*Supper*

3rd Day, May 30—Diagnosis and Action

8:00-10:00 a.m.	*The Board Membership Process*
10:00-10:15	*Break*
10:15-12:30	*Diagnosis and Action*
12:30 p.m.	*Closing Remarks*
3:00 p.m.	*Check-Out Time*

Figure 11-12. (Also on facing page) Orientation flow and assignments

NEWPORT ORGANIZATION

ONE DAY CONFERENCE ON BOARDS

Purpose: 1. To provide orientation to Board Organization and Board Membership.

2. To provide a forum for the exchange of ideas and concerns between Corporate and Unit Boards.

James L. Curtis
Conference Chairperson

11:00 a.m.	Registration
11:30 a.m.	Luncheon—Monroe Room
12:30 p.m.	General Session—The Voluntary Concept

	Presiding:	James L. Curtis, Chairperson Resource Development Committee
	Public Relations Program:	Herbert Lunn, Chairperson Public Relations Committee
	Speaker:	Eliott P. Sampson, Chairperson Newport Organization "The Organization of the Newport Organization"

Split Sessions on Standing Committee Purpose and Function

1:00-1:45 p.m.	*Room A—Program Services Committee Chairperson: Herman S. Schmidt*
1:50-2:35 p.m.	*Room B—Resource Development Committee Chairperson: Lloyd M. Tully*
2:55-3:40 p.m.	*Room C—Business Committee Chairperson: William C. Pierce*
3:45-4:30 p.m.	*Room D—Personnel Committee Chairperson: Rodney T. Pratt*

Each Color Group will have a 45 minute session with each Standing Committee. There will be a 20 minute coffee break at 2:35 p.m.

Color groups will move as follows:

Red   A — B — C — D
Blue   B — C — D — A
Green   C — D — A — B
Purple   D — A — B — C

4:40-5:20	*Wrap-Up Panel to Respond to Questions of Conferees—Monroe Room* *Closing Remarks—Eliott P. Sampson*
5:30 p.m.	*Cocktails (Cash Bar)—Monroe Room*

A new board volunteer will feel considerably more comfortable once the first assignment has been given. A sense of participation and achievement is always greatest in a small sphere of work that is close to the volunteer's own skills and knowledge. Broader organizational understanding can come later.

The best way is to have a board or staff team lead an orientation for several people at once. Since people tend to join boards at different times, however, it makes little sense to delay an orientation until there are four or five people ready. Board volunteers may even receive orientation programs after they have already served six to eight months; it is better, however, to hold the orientation session within a week of recruitment. Some organizations give the orientation in one large block of time; others will segment it. Whatever method is selected, orientation must be done well.

We recommend that a prospect not agree to stand for election until after undergoing orientation. Orientation is really another screen. It is possible that a prospect may agree to recruitment, but become disinterested after orientation. It is better to detach deadwood as early as possible. If a prospect refuses orientation, it is doubtful that the prospect would have been a good board volunteer anyway.

Continuing Education

Recruitment, orientation, and continuing education all overlap. When a prospect is being recruited, the individual is, in a sense, being oriented and is also receiving an education. Once the prospect agrees to or declines recruitment, the recruitment phase ends. After orientation is concluded, the new board volunteer participates in continuing education for the entire period of his or her service.

Formal continuing education includes the programs or meetings which are specifically set up for that purpose. These may include sessions conducted by the organization or sessions conducted *outside* the organization which are attended by board members.

Informal continuing education isn't specifically planned, but takes place within the framework of processes, meetings, and programs set up for purposes other than continuing education, such as meetings called to conduct the work of the board and interactions among board volunteers, staff, clients, and community.

The formal continuing education processes are vital because they directly affect the efficacy of the informal processes. The less data available from the formal network, the more the informal network thrives on misinformation, misconceptions, misrepresentations, and mischief.

Finally, although not strictly a part of continuing education, it is vital to an organization that a climate of belonging be established among board volunteers. It is better if the staff knows the volunteers and considers them more than mere instruments. Little things such as an occasional thank-you note for work well done or congratulations on special occasions are in order.

Members of an organization often ask board volunteers for their help; then they tend to whitewash problems for them, do their work for them (if it gets done at all), do their thinking for them (as if they were *non compos mentis*), feed them a steady diet of baffling and/or dull statistics (as if they wouldn't understand the really important issues), and avoid all controversy in meetings (lest they learn something both from and about them, or have their own pet ideas challenged). Continuing education is the key to avoiding this situation.

12

Bylaws

An organization's articles of incorporation are those documents, filed with the state, upon which the organization's corporate not-for-profit status is granted. How often do most organizations pull these documents out of the safe for examination? Some organizations have never examined their legal documents— or the last they did so was far too long ago. In the interim, many things in the organization may have changed that might have required corresponding changes in the articles of incorporation. The point is, these documents must be examined on a periodic basis. This demonstrates board diligence.

As previously mentioned, we live in an increasingly litigious society. Nonprofit organizations must be certain that all legal documents, minutes of meetings, annual reports, and financials are in proper order and that the requirements of local, state, and federal statutes are being followed. The bylaws of an organization are an important document and can play a part in any suit brought against the organization.

The bylaws are the documents through which the voluntary organization operates. If a staff member or board volunteer has a question about the organization or about a function of the organization, the bylaws serve as the final arbiter. They can be amended or changed only by action of the board of directors.

A word of caution to staff members: One of the easiest traps to fall into is to modify or change your organization in some way without first seeking the required approval from the board of directors. The bylaws are your basic operating policies. Don't ignore or neglect them. Treat them with due respect.

Our model, the Newport Organization, has four units, each of which has a board of managers. Hence, there are board of managers bylaws that govern the operation of each unit.

Here is, at a minimum, what every set of bylaws should cover:

1. Statement of purpose
2. Description of the voting membership (board members)
3. Tenure of service
4. Number of meetings
5. Number and description of standing committees
6. Description and responsibilities of executive committee
7. Election of officers
8. Terms of officers
9. Appointment of committee chairperson
10. Tenure of chairperson
11. Annual meeting
12. Quorums
13. Filling of vacancies
14. Employment of staff
15. Amendments
16. Special meetings
17. Required reports
18. Removal of officers
19. Statement of fiscal year
20. Bank accounts, deposits, and disbursement of funds
21. Conflict of interest
22. Indemnification
23. Parliamentary authority

No single set of bylaws can be written for all organizations. There are, however, certain basic components, as listed above, that are applicable to all. Bylaws are governed by state statutes, the requirements of which must be observed most scrupulously. The following bylaws are merely a sample of the types of articles that are widely used. The content can vary greatly, and additional articles may be added. Each organization should retain an attorney to draft bylaws specific to the needs of that organization.

Bylaws of Newport Organization
ARTICLE I
Purposes

The purposes of this corporation, as stated in its Articles of Incorporation, are exclusively charitable and educational and solely in furtherance thereof:

The purposes of the corporation, as stated in its certificate of incorporation, are the education, guidance, physical well-being and training of boys and girls and, in furtherance thereof, the maintenance and operation of clubs, clubhouses, camps, farms, and other facilities and the conduction of classes, courses, and activities in connection therewith, without regard to race, creed, or national origin.

No part of the net earnings of the corporation shall inure to the benefit of any private individual, no part of the activities of the corporation shall be carrying on propaganda or otherwise attempting to influence legislation, and the corporation shall not participate in, or intervene in (including the publishing or distributing of statements) any political campaign on behalf of any candidate for public office.

Upon dissolution of this corporation, all of its net assets shall be distributed to such charitable and educational organizations, as described in section 501(c)(3) of the Internal Revenue Code of 1954, and similar sections of future laws, as the directors in their sole discretion shall determine.

ARTICLE II

The corporation shall maintain in the State a registered office and a registered agent at such office, and may have other offices within or without the state.

ARTICLE III
Board of Directors

3.1 GENERAL POWERS. The affairs of the corporation shall be managed by its board of directions (Board).

3.2 NUMBER, TENURE AND QUALIFICATION. The number of directors shall be not fewer than 7. Beginning at the organizational meeting held in 1978, one-third of the Board shall be elected for a term of one year, one-third for a term of two years, and one-third for a term of three years and thereafter each director shall be elected for a term of three years and until successors shall have been elected. Directors shall be elected by directors at an annual meeting. Directors need not be residents.

3.3 REGULAR MEETINGS. A regular annual meeting of the Board shall be held each year without notice other than these bylaws, on the first Monday in March at the hour of 12:00 noon at the registered office of the corporation, or at such other time and place as the Board shall select. The board shall provide by resolution for the holding of additional regular meetings which may be held without notice other than by such resolution. The Board shall meet at least once each calendar quarter.

3.4 SPECIAL MEETINGS. Special meetings of the Board may be called by the Chairperson or any two directors. The persons calling special meetings may fix the place for holding any special meeting called by them.

3.5 NOTICE. Written notice of any special meeting shall be given to each director at least forty-eight hours in advance at the director's address shown in the corporate records. If mailed, notice shall be deemed delivered when deposited in the United States mail, postage prepaid, in a sealed addressed envelope. Notice of any special meeting may be waived in writing signed either before or after the meeting by the persons entitled to notice. The attendance of a director at any meeting shall waive notice of such meeting, except where a director attends a meeting for the express purpose of objecting to the transaction of business because the meeting is not lawfully called. The business to be transacted at, or the purpose of, any regular or special meeting need not be specified in the notice or waiver of notice of such meeting, unless specifically required by law or by these bylaws. A meeting attended by all directors of the corporation shall be a valid meeting without notice.

3.6 QUORUM. One-third of the directors shall constitute a quorum for the transaction of business, provided that if less than one-third of the directors are present at any meeting, a majority of directors present may adjourn the meeting to another time without further notice.

3.7 MANNER OF ACTING. The act of a majority of directors

present at a meeting at which a quorum is present shall be the act of the Board, unless the act of a greater number is required by statute or by the bylaws.

3.8 INFORMAL ACTION BY DIRECTORS. Any action required to be taken, or which may be taken, at a meeting of directors, may be taken without a meeting if a written consent setting forth the action taken is signed by all of the directors entitled to vote with respect to the action.

3.9 CONFLICT OF INTEREST. Any possible conflict of interest on the part of a director shall be disclosed to the Board. When any such interest becomes a matter of Board action, such director shall not vote or use personal influence on the matter, and shall not be counted in the quorum for a meeting at which Board action is to be taken on the interest. The Director may, however, briefly state a position on the matter and answer pertinent questions of Board members. The minutes of all actions taken on such matters shall clearly reflect that these requirements have been met.

3.10 VACANCIES. Any vacancy occurring in the Board or any directorship to be filled by reason of an increase in the number of directors shall be filled by the Board. A director elected to fill a vacancy shall be elected for the remaining term of the director's predecessor in office.

3.11 COMPENSATION. Directors shall not receive any salaries for their services, but by resolution of the Board, expenses of attendance may be allowed for each regular or special meeting.

ARTICLE IV
Officers

4.1 OFFICERS. The officers of the corporation are Chairperson of the Board, vice chairperson-program, vice chairperson-resource development, vice chairperson and treasurer-business, vice chairperson-personnel, secretary, and such assistant treasurers, assistant secretaries or other officers as may be elected by the Board. Officers whose authority and duties are not prescribed in the bylaws shall have such authority and duties as prescribed by the Board. Any two or more offices may be held by the same person, except the offices of Chairperson and secretary.

4.2 ELECTION AND TERM OF OFFICE. The officers shall be elected annually by the Board at its annual meeting. The Chairperson, vice chairperson and secretary shall be elected from among members of the Board; the president shall not be a member of the Board.

4.3 REMOVAL. Any officer may be removed by the Board whenever in its judgment the best interest of the corporation would be served, but without prejudice to the contract rights, if any, of the officer.

4.4 CHAIRPERSON. The Chairperson shall be the principal executive officer of the corporation. Subject to the direction and control of the Board, the Chairperson shall see that the resolutions and directives of the Board are carried into effect; and, in general, shall discharge all duties incident to the office of Chairperson and as prescribed by the Board. The Chairperson shall preside at all meetings of the Board. Except in those instances in which the authority to execute is expressly delegated to another officer or agent of the corporation, or a different mode of execution is expressly prescribed by the Board, the Chairperson may execute for the corporation any contracts, deeds, mortgages, bonds, or other instruments which the Board has authorized either individually or attested to by the secretary, an assistant secretary, or any other officer, according to the requirements of the instrument. The Chairperson may vote all securities which the corporation is entitled to vote except to the extent a different corporate officer or agent is authorized by the Board.

4.5 VICE CHAIRPERSON. The vice chairperson shall assist the Chairperson in the discharge of the Chairperson's duties as the Chairperson may direct and shall perform such other duties as may be assigned by the Chairperson or by the Board. Vice chairpersons are elected by the Board from a slate recommended by the Chairperson. In the event of absence, inability, or refusal of the Chairperson to act, the vice chairperson in the order designated below, shall perform the duties of the Chairperson with all the power of, and subject to all the restrictions upon the Chairperson.

4.6a VICE CHAIRPERSON-PROGRAM. The vice chairperson-program shall serve as chairperson of the Program Committee and shall perform such other duties as may be assigned by the Chairperson or by the Board.

4.6b VICE CHAIRPERSON-RESOURCE DEVELOPMENT. The vice chairperson-resource development shall serve as chairperson of the Resource Development Committee and shall perform such other duties as may be assigned by the Chairperson or by the Board.

4.6c VICE CHAIRPERSON AND TREASURER-BUSINESS. The vice chairperson and treasurer-business shall be the principal accounting and financial officer of the corporation and shall be responsible for the maintenance of adequate corporate books of account; have charge and custody of all corporate funds and securities, and be responsible for the receipt and disbursement thereof; shall serve as chairperson of the Business Committee; and perform all the duties incident to the office of treasurer and such other duties as may be assigned by the Chairperson or by the Board. If required by the Board, the treasurer shall give a bond for the faithful discharge of duties in such sum and form as the Board shall determine.

4.6d VICE CHAIRPERSON-PERSONNEL. The vice chairperson-personnel shall serve as chairperson of the Personnel Committee and shall perform such other duties as may be assigned by the Chairperson or by the Board.

4.7 SECRETARY. The secretary shall record the minutes of the meetings of the Board; see that notices are given in accordance with the bylaws or as required by law; keep the corporate records and seal; keep a register of the address furnished to the secretary by each member; and perform all duties incident to the office of secretary and such other duties as may be assigned by the Chairperson or by the Board.

4.8 ASSISTANT TREASURERS AND ASSISTANT SECRETARIES. The assistant treasurers and assistant secretaries shall perform such duties as shall be assigned to them by the treasurer or the secretary, respectively, or by the Chairperson or the Board. If required by the Board, the assistant treasurers shall give bond for the faithful discharge of their duties in such sum and form as the Board shall determine.

ARTICLE V
Employed Staff

5.1 EXECUTIVE DIRECTOR. The Board shall employ an Executive Director who shall be the chief operational officer of the corporation. Subject to the Board, the Executive Director shall have general direction over the operations of the corporation; shall implement all policies of the Board; shall submit to the Board or its committees such reports as the Board may require; shall assist in the preparation of an annual budget for presentation to and adoption by the Board; shall assist in the preparation of a personnel policy; provide staff support to the Board; and shall perform such other functions as the Board may direct. The Executive Director shall be responsible directly to the Board of Directors and shall attend all meetings of the Board and its committees without vote.

5.2 OTHER STAFF. Such employed staff as may be necessary to support the organization shall be hired and discharged by the Executive Director. The employed staff shall report directly to, and be accountable to, the Executive Director or his or her designates.

ARTICLE VI
Committees

6.1 EXECUTIVE COMMITTEE. The Executive Committee shall consist of the Chairperson, the vice chairperson, secretary, and two directors elected annually by the Board. The responsibility of the Executive Committee is to direct the planning function. It has no authority to act in the name of the Board of Directors.

6.2 STANDING COMMITTEES. The corporation shall have the following standing committees which shall be advisory to the Board: Program Committee, Resource Development Committee, Finance Committee, and Human Resources Committee. Members of standing committees shall be appointed by the Board. A majority of members of each standing committee shall be directors. The duties of the standing committees shall be adopted by the board.

6.3 OTHER COMMITTEES. Other committees not exercising the authority of the Board may be designated by a resolution adopted by a majority of directors present at a meeting at which a quorum is present. Except as otherwise provided in such resolution, the Chairperson of the corporation shall appoint and remove committee members whenever the best interests of the corporation are served thereby.

6.4 TERM OF OFFICE. Each committee member shall serve until the next annual meeting of the corporation and until a successor is appointed, unless the member is removed from, or ceases to qualify as, a member of the committee, or unless the committee is sooner terminated.

6.5 VACANCIES. Vacancies in the membership of any committee may be filled by appointments made in the same manner as in the case of the original appointments.

6.6 QUORUM. Unless otherwise provided in the resolution designating a committee, a majority of the committee shall constitute a quorum and the act of a majority of the members present at a meeting at which a quorum is present shall be the act of the committee.

6.7 RULES. Each committee may adopt governing rules not inconsistent with these bylaws or with rules adopted by the Board.

ARTICLE VII
Indemnification as Needed

7.1 INSURANCE. The corporation may purchase and maintain insurance on behalf of any person who may be indemnified here against any liability asserted against such person and incurred in any capacity, or arising out of any status, for which the person may be indemnified.

ARTICLE VIII
Miscellaneous

8.1 CONTRACTS. The Board may authorize any officer or agent of the corporation, in addition to the officers authorized by the bylaws, to enter into any contract or execute and deliver any instrument in the name of, and on behalf of, the corporation. Such authority may be general or confined to specific instanced.

8.2 CHECKS, DRAFTS, Etc. All orders for the payment of money, or evidences of indebtedness issued in the name of the corporation, shall be signed by such corporate officer or agent as the Board shall determine. In the absence of such a determination, such instruments shall be signed by the treasurer or an assistant treasurer and countersigned by the Chairperson or a vice chairperson.

8.3 DEPOSITS. All corporate funds shall be deposited to the credit of the corporation in such banks or other depositaries as the Board may select.

8.4 GIFTS. The Board may accept on behalf of the corporation any contribution, gift, bequest or devise for the general, or for any special, corporate purpose.

8.5 RECORDS. The corporation shall keep, at the registered or principal office, complete books of account, minutes of the proceedings of directors and committees having any authority of the Board, and a record with the names and addresses of directors. All corporate records may be inspected by any director, or the director's agent or attorney for any proper purpose at any reasonable time.

8.6 FISCAL YEAR. The fiscal year of the corporation shall end on December 31 of each year.

8.7 SEAL. The corporate seal shall have inscribed on it the name of the corporation and the words "Corporate Seal, Illinois."

8.8 WAIVER OF NOTICE. Whenever any notice is required to be given, a waiver in writing signed by the persons entitled to such notice, whether before or after the time stated therein, shall be deemed equivalent to the giving of notice.

ARTICLE IX
Amendments

The bylaws may be altered, amended, or repealed or new bylaws adopted by affirmative vote of a majority of the Board. Such action may be taken at any regular or special meeting of the Board for which notice of the proposed action shall have been given in accordance with the bylaws.

ARTICLE X
Parliamentary Authority

The rules contained in *Robert's Rules of Order, Newly Revised,* shall govern the Newport Organization in all cases wherein they are not superseded by the bylaws or special rules of order.

ARTICLE XI

[Some organizations have unit operations. This article would apply to these situations.]

Operation of Units

The Board of Managers of each Unit is established by the Board of Directors and shall at all times be subject to the direction of the President of the Corporation. The Unit Director shall at all times be subject to the direction of the President of the Corporation through the Executive Director.

The Board of Managers shall be responsible for the management of the affairs of such Units, subject to the limitation of these bylaws and the Board of Managers bylaws. All action of the Board of Managers shall be subject to the approval of the Board of Directors, shall meet no fewer than six (6) times annually, and the annual business meeting shall be in November of each year. The nominee for the Chairmanship of the Board of Managers shall be presented to the

Nominating Committee of the Board of Directors. The Chairman of the Board of Managers shall be a member of the Board of Directors and shall serve on the Board of Directors during his term of office as such Chairman. He shall also serve on the Executive Committee. Such Board of Managers, insofar as may be feasible, shall be constituted of persons living or conducting business establishments in or about the neighborhood of such Unit. The Board of Managers shall be evaluated annually. The rules and bylaws pertaining to the management and operation of each Unit shall be such as may be prescribed from time to time by the Board of Directors of the Corporation. The Board of Directors of the Corporation any likewise appoint, or authorize the President of the Corporation to appoint, such other persons as may be necessary to operate and supervise any such Unit.

13

Committee Commissions

In chapter 6, I discussed the work of committees. A committee's "work" comes from the goals and objectives that fall within its jurisdiction. In addition to these goals and objectives, there should be a "committee commission" for each committee that describes its function. These commissions generally have three parts:

General commission:	A general description of the committee's work and its authority
Appointments and composition:	Who is on the committee and who appoints members
Responsibilities:	The committee's assigned tasks that must correspond with the Work to Be Done II chart

The following are examples of committee commissions. There are many other models, but this is my preference.

Executive Committee Commission

General Commission

The executive committee is commissioned by and responsible to the board of directors of the Newport Organization to function on behalf of the board of directors in matters of emergency and in interim periods between regularly scheduled Board meetings. The executive committee shall have and exercise the authority of the board of directors, provided that such authority shall not operate to circumvent the responsibility and authority vested in the board of directors by the Newport Organization's bylaws or the exceptions noted in this commission.

Appointments and Composition

1. The executive committee shall be composed of the officers of the board of directors and the chairpersons of all standing committees.
2. Chairpersons of ad hoc committees may be appointed by the board chairperson for the duration of the committee function.
3. Immediate past officers of the board may be appointed to the executive committee at the discretion of the board chairperson.
4. The executive director is ex-officio member of the executive committee.
5. Others as needed.

Responsibilities

1. Respond to the call of the board chairperson or executive director for emergency meetings to deal with special problems between regular board meetings.
2. Meet during those months when no regular board meetings are held to deal with ongoing, organizational concerns.
3. Review quarterly all committee reports to assure relevant board meeting agenda and to bring to the attention of the board any problems which might otherwise escape action.
4. The executive committee may not act on matters of finance, executive director, property, contracts, or bylaws.

Finance Committee Commission

General Commission

The finance committee is commissioned by and responsible to the board of directors of the Newport Organization to assume the primary relationship in matters pertaining to the Newport Organization's purposes, maintain quality programs and services, and perform the following functions subject to and in conformity with established policies of the Newport Organization and the approval of the board of directors.

Appointments and Composition

1. Appointments to the finance committee are made in December of each year by the chairperson of the board for the following fiscal year.
2. The finance committee shall include a chairperson, the treasurer of the board of directors, and a minimum of three other board of directors members.
3. Additional members may be appointed from the board of directors as needed and according to particular ability.

Responsibilities

1. Appoint and supervise the investment committee which has the responsibility for the endowment and investment portfolios.
2. Appoint and supervise the property committee which has responsibility for the physical facilities.
3. Participate in the preparation of the organization's budget as outlined in the corporate budgeting process.
4. Review monthly finance reports received from accounting and report to the board of directors on the financial operation.
5. Control current financial operations within the limit of the total approved budget.
6. Prepare for the board of directors meeting at the beginning of each calendar quarter a financial projection for the current year and make appropriate recommendations concerning necessary actions to achieve a balanced budget.
7. Organize and establish such subcommittees as may be required to further its work and fulfill its function.

Resource Development Committee Commission

General Commission

The resource development committee is commissioned by and responsible to the board of directors of the Newport Organization to assume the primary relationship in matters pertaining to campaign, public relations, planned giving, and board membership in accordance with the established policies and practices approved by the board of directors of the Newport Organization.

Appointments and Composition

1. The chairperson of the resource development committee is appointed by the chairperson of the board.
2. The resource development committee is composed of the chairperson and vice chairperson of the resource development committee and the chairpersons of the subcommittees on campaign, board membership, public relations, planned giving, and capital giving. Other members can be appointed as deemed necessary.

Responsibilities

1. Supervise the functions of its subcommittees.
2. Participate in the budget process of the organization as outlined in that process.
3. Ensure that the subcommittees of the respective resource development committees meet on a regular basis and achieve their goals and objectives.

Human Resource Committee Commission

General Commission

The human resource committee is commissioned by and responsible to the board of directors of the Newport Organization to assume the responsibility for advising it on matters pertaining to human resource administration and staffing of the units, so that all functions of the organization may be effectively and efficiently carried forth in conformity with the established policies and practices approved by the board of directors of the Newport Organization.

Appointments and Composition

1. Appointments to the human resource committee are made on an annual basis by the chairperson of the board of directors for the ensuing year.
2. The human resource committee shall have sixteen members. The human resource committee may include members not on the board of directors.

Responsibilities

1. Provide overall policy guidance for human resource operations in the Newport Organization.
2. Submit, for final approval, recommendations on personnel policy matters to the executive committee of the board of Directors.
3. Provide general supervision of personnel operations in the areas of:
   a. Policy revision
   b. Salary administration
   c. Fringe benefits administration
   d. Staff development and training
   e. Recruitment and retention
   f. Employee relations
4. Review, with the executive director, the staffing design of the organization for the coming year.
5. The chairperson of the personnel committee serves, with other committee chairpersons, on an ad hoc budget committee to recommend salaries.
6. Review staff additions and terminations and make periodic reports to the board of directors on the general state of staff capability for the meeting of the Newport Organization's objectives.

Program Services Committee Commission

General Commission

The program services committee has the primary responsibility for the overall program emphasis of the Newport Organization. It shall develop programs and monitor program goals with the involvement of the total organization.

Appointments and Composition

1. Appointments to the program services committee will be made by the chairperson of the board of directors on an annual basis with the advice and consent of the chairperson of the program services committee for the ensuing year.
2. The committee shall consist of sixteen members.
3. Any number of subcommittees may be appointed, and non-board members may be appointed to serve.

Responsibilities

1. Meet on the fourth Tuesday in the months of March, June, September, and December.
2. Develop program services action goals, both long and short term.
3. Plan and develop services and monitor the progress toward the stated objectives.
4. Evaluate shifts in program services with emphasis on the necessary recommendations for policy changes.
5. Evaluate services.
6. Appraise jointly with the resource development committee those increases and decreases which involve financing, for suitable recommendations to the executive committee.
7. Support and enhance the existing program of the Newport Organization by bringing to it new resources and ideas. This can be accomplished by program services committee members' serving on the subcommittees of the Newport Organization.
8. Evaluate and recommend new programs to the board in line with the purpose and objectives of the Newport Organization. This function will be carried out by the program services committee as new major programs are recommended by professional staff or lay boards. The program services committee evaluates the suggested new programs and makes its recommendations to the executive committee of the board of directors.
9. Interpret the program services of the Newport Organization to the board of directors of the Newport Organization in order that members of the board are aware of, and understand, these services. This may be accomplished by means of the following:
   a. Special tours of organization's facilities by the board, sponsored by the program services committee.
   b. Special program presentations in board meetings.
   c. Special printed materials which the board would receive from time to time, informing them of current program serviced.
10. Recommend facility expansion, reduction, and repair of program areas.

Commission for a Property Subcommittee of the Finance Committee

General Commission

The property subcommittee is commissioned by and responsible to the finance committee to assume the primary relationship to matters pertaining to building care and maintenance, protecting the capital investment of the Newport Organization in buildings and grounds, and assuring the functional utility of all areas and equipment.

Appointments and Composition

1. Appointments to the property subcommittee are made on an annual basis by the chairperson of the board of managers and the chairperson of the finance committee for the ensuing year.
2. The chairperson of this subcommittee is to be a member of the finance committee.
3. Other members may be appointed from the community in accordance with particular capacities in specialized fields.
4. These members will be appointed by the board chairperson and the finance committee chairperson upon recommendation of the property committee chairperson.

Responsibilities

1. Make a complete inspection and evaluation of building condition, noting all maintenance and repair needs of the Unit, in April of each year.
2. Develop a schedule for the completion of all needed heavy maintenance during the summer months.
3. Develop a schedule for routine and prevention maintenance, e.g., painting, boiler and equipment care.
4. Make a monthly inspection of the building and meet with the executive director for purposes of consultation and making suggestions relative to performance of maintenance staff.
5. Appoint one member of the subcommittee who will give regular attention to housekeeping, safety, and sanitation aspects of the building, and maintain communication with the unit director.
6. Make brief written monthly reports for the board of directors.
7. Create and review risk management program annually.

8. Scrutinize gas, electric, chemical, and cleaning-supply consumption in relation to budget and areas of possible waste.
9. Prepare, by May of each year, an estimated budget of spending necessary within this department, for study and incorporation into the Unit budget.
10. Anticipate any major maintenance problems for which special financing may be necessary, and notify the finance committee so that provisions can be made. Provide estimated costs with this report.

Commission for a Board Membership Subcommittee of the Resource Development Committee

General Commission

The board membership subcommittee is commissioned by and responsible to the resource development committee of unit one of the Newport Organization to assume the primary relationship to matters pertaining to board of managers' recruitment, orientation, motivation, and evaluation in accordance with established policies and practices approved by the corporate board of the Newport Organization.

Appointments and Composition

1. The appointment of the chairperson of the board membership subcommittee is to be made by the chairperson of the resource development committee for the ensuing year. This appointment is to be made in consultation with the chairperson of the board.
2. Other members of this committee are to be selected at a meeting of the board chairperson, resource development committee chairperson, and the board membership subcommittee chairperson.

Responsibilities

1. Study the composition of the board, having in mind optimum breadth of talents, skills, and capacity to assume all aspects of the unit's success.
2. Ongoing evaluation of the present board of managers, always asking "How can the talents of this person be better challenged for the benefit of unit one?" Keep an ongoing record of board meeting attendance, committee service, and evidence of commitment to the youth of Newport.

3. Prepare an annual program for board in-service training and volunteer recognition.
4. Nominate for the board service such candidates as have a real contribution to make to the success of the unit.
5. Poll the board annually as to the areas of committee service each is best fitted for.
6. Review annually the procedures for board recruitment.

Commission for a Public Relations Subcommittee of the Resource Development Committee

General Commission

The public relations subcommittee is commissioned by and is responsible to the resource development committee of unit one of the Newport Organization to assume the primary relationship to matters pertaining to public relations and publicity, enhancing the internal and external image of the Newport Organization in the area served by the unit, and coordinating all matters pertaining to public relations and publicity with the department of resource development in the administrative office of the Newport Organization.

Appointments and Composition

1. Appointments to the public relations subcommittee are made on an annual basis by the chairperson of the resource development committee for the ensuing year.
2. The chairperson of this subcommittee is to be a member of the board of directors.
3. Other members may be appointed from the community in accordance with particular capacity in specialized fields, with particular emphasis on persons with experience in the field of public relations or related areas of communication.
4. These members will be appointed by the board chairperson and the resource development committee chairperson upon recommendation of the public relations subcommittee chairperson.

Responsibilities

1. Develop a complete program of public relations, promotion, and publicity projected for a one-year basis beginning each April.
2. Establish and maintain a good working relationship with the media.

3. Develop a routine of coverage and information built around news events pertaining to organization.
4. Maintain a liaison with the department of resource development for the Newport Organization in developing and instituting long-range public relations programs.

14

Manuals of Operation for Committees

Manuals of operation are designed to assist a committee in the performance of its duties, providing reference materials and detailed procedures. The following is a sample of the contents of a manual of operation for a nominating committee.

Interpretive Index

Commission for the Nominating Committee (Ad Hoc)

This is the job description for your committee, spelling out your responsibilities and your place in the accountability pattern.

Criteria for Board Member Performance Evaluation

Board membership within the Newport Organization system involves a heavy and serious commitment. Evaluation criteria are necessary to determine whether or not a member should be asked to remain after his or her three-year term has expired.

Board Member Meeting and Activity Record

This recording sheet indicates the degree of participation of each board member and should be considered, along with other factors, in the renomination of Board personnel.

Board of Directors Individual Contribution Record

One important function of a member of the Board of Directors is helping to finance the work.

Master Schedule of Board and Committee Meetings

This is an index of total lay participation.

Annual Performance Evaluation of Board Members for Use of Nominating Committee

This is the recommendation of your committee regarding nomination and serves as the basis for Board action.

Nomination of Officers

Nominating of officers follows normal procedure in accordance with criteria.

Commission for the Nominating Committee.

To: The Nominating Committee (ad hoc)
From: The Board of Directors

General Commission

The Nominating Committee is commissioned by and responsible to the Board of Directors of the Newport Organization to prepare a single slate of all officers and members of the Board of Directors whose terms expire and to file such slate with the Executive Director no later than thirty (30) days prior to the November business meeting.

Appointments and Composition

1. The Nominating Committee is elected in September of each year.
2. The Committee is composed of members of the Board of Directors whose terms of office do not expire in that given year.
3. The Committee, at its first meeting, will elect a Chairperson.

Responsibilities

To evaluate carefully the performance of each Board member, recommend candidates for office, and prepare a slate of members for retention on the Board or to be dropped from the Board.

Criteria for Board Member Performance Evaluation
Newport Organization Nominating Committee

The success of the Newport Organization is based on the participation of its laymen. It is therefore crucial that the performance of each layman

NEWPORT ORGANIZATION

BOARD OF DIRECTORS

MASTER SCHEDULE OF BOARD AND COMMITTEE MEETINGS

YEAR 20__

MEETINGS		JAN.	FEB.	MAR.	APR.	MAY	JUNE	JULY	AUG	SEPT.	OCT.	NOV.	DEC.	MEETING TOTAL
BOARD														
COMMITTEES														
1. EXECUTIVE														
2. PROGRAM SERVICES														
3.														
4.														
5.														
6.														
7. RESOURCE DEVELOPMENT														
8. CAMPAIGN														
9. MEMBERSHIP														
10. PUBLIC RELATIONS														
11. FINANCE														
12. PROPERTY														
13. PERSONNEL														
14.														
15.														
MONTHLY TOTAL														

Figure 14–1. Master schedule of board and committee meetings

NEWPORT ORGANIZATION

BOARD MEMBER MEETING AND ACTIVITY RECORD

NAME_____

UNIT_____   DATE ELECTED TO BOARD_____

MEETINGS		JAN.	FEB.	MAR.	APR.	MAY	JUNE	JULY	AUG.	SEPT.	OCT.	NOV.	DEC.	MEETINGS HELD	TOTAL ATTENDED
BOARD															
COMMITTEES															
1.															
2.															
3.															
4.															
CORPORATE MEETINGS ATTENDED															
SPECIAL EVENT PARTICIPATION															

OFFICES HELD	NEW BOARD MEMBERS RECRUITED	PROGRAMS OR SERVICES INITIATED	OTHER ACTIVITIES
_____	_____	_____	_____
_____	_____	_____	_____
_____	_____	_____	_____
_____	_____	_____	_____

Meeting Record: If board member attends, place date of meeting in under month.
Total number of meetings held is obtained from the Board and Committee
Meeting form.

Figure 14–2. Board member meeting and activity record

	CAMPAIGN									
YEAR	PERSONAL	COMPANY	RAISED	UNITS	WOMEN'S BOARD	SPECIAL EVENTS COMMITTEE	MATERIAL	NON-OPERATING	WILLS & BEQUESTS	TOTAL

NEWPORT ORGANIZATION

BOARD OF DIRECTORS INDIVIDUAL CONTRIBUTION RECORD

NAME_____ UNIT_____ MEMBER SINCE_____

Figure 14–3. Board of directors individual contribution record

NEWPORT ORGANIZATION

ANNUAL PERFORMANCE EVALUATION OF BOARD MEMBERS FOR USE OF NOMINATING COMMITTEE

SUBMITTED TO BOARD OF DIRECTORS BY_____, CHAIRMAN   DATE_____

NAME	MEMBER SINCE	ACTION TAKEN		
		UNQUALIFIED RENOMINATION	PROGRAMMED RENOMINATION	PROGRAMMED SEPARATION

Figure 14–4. Annual performance evaluation of board members for use of nominating committee

NEWPORT ORGANIZATION

REPORT ON NOMINATION OF OFFICERS

Chairman of Board: _____

President: _____

Vice Presidents: _____

_____

_____

_____

_____

_____

Secretary: _____

Treasurer: _____

Other:

_____

_____

_____

_____

_____

_____

(To be submitted to Executive Director)

Figure 14–5. Nomination of officers

be evaluated by the Nominating Committee. Listed below are some suggested criteria for evaluating a Board member's performance:

1. Participation in fund raising
2. Material contributions
3. Board meetings attended
4. Committee meetings attended
5. Participation on ad hoc committees
6. Offices held
7. Recruitment of new Board members
8. Innovative ideas introduced

It is not possible to set uniform standards which fit all situations. Nominating committees, therefore, should weigh each criterion according to its conditions.

Board Evaluation Forms

1. Master schedule of Board and committee meetings—Form 1.
2. Board member meeting and activity record—Form 2.
3. Board of Directors individual contribution record—Form 3.
4. Annual performance evaluation of Board members for use of Nominating Committee—Form 4.
5. Nomination of officers—Form 5.

Section V

How a Board Operates

15

Communication and Motivation

Motivation

How selfish soever man may be supposed, there are evidently some principles in his nature, which interest him in the fortune of others, and render their happiness necessary to him, though he derives nothing from it, except the pleasure of seeing it.

—Adam Smith, *Theory of Moral Sentiments,* 1759

What turns a board member on? Two of my classes asked more than one hundred board members why they became more involved with their organizations. We found that most board volunteers described a passage through clearly definable stages of interest. Obviously not every board volunteer went through every stage. A large number of them, however, did pass through the spectrum of interest, allowing us to form what we call the involvement/contribution ratio:

A board volunteer's contribution to his or her organization increases in direct proportion to his or her involvement. This suggests that involvement goes through definable stages over relative time periods.

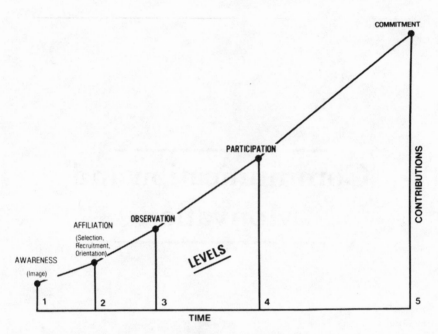

Figure 15-1. Involvement-contribution ratio

The perpendicular axis in Figure 15-1 refers to contributions—not only in dollars, but in time, in attendance at meetings, and in willingness to contribute company facilities and equipment. The horizontal axis refers to the relative length of time it takes a board volunteer to reach each level. Remember that this ratio is not a scientific measurement, but merely a tool to use in describing how board volunteers develop.

Level 1: Awareness

A prospective board member may not be aware of the organization. If the prospect is indeed aware of its existence, then he or she has developed an image of the organization. If that image is positive or neutral, affiliation is possible. If it is negative, chances are slim that affiliation will occur.

Level 2: Affiliation

In terms of the board membership process, this phase corresponds to selection, recruitment, and orientation. If affiliation is handled well, the stage has been set for a developing board volunteer. This is the new board member's first and most important impression of the organization. At this point, a willingness to contribute is exhibited.

Level 3: Observation

The new board member now makes a critical decision. By observing the organization in action, the new board member will either find that the organization's practice has met the promise of recruitment and orientation or that it doesn't measure up. If the organization does not measure up, the new board member is almost inevitably and irretrievably lost. If the organization does measure up to those early expectations, the board member moves to the next level.

Level 4: Participation

At this level, the board volunteer finds that he or she has meaningful work to do. The board volunteer discovers that his or her participation is useful and can make a difference. Contributions go up.

Level 5: Commitment

This is the final stage—the stage of the board volunteer's commitment to the cause or purpose of the organization. This is the culmination of belief in the cause with solid leadership. From this point on, the board volunteer is self-motivated. For example, I know of a board member whose company went bankrupt. He had signed a $250,000 pledge for a new building, and rather than renege on that obligation, he sold a portion of his farm to meet this commitment. In another memorable case, a board member had lost a considerable amount of money in an economic recession and found that she had to cut back on her charitable contributions. She cut back on all her contributions except one—the one she was really committed to. In fact, she doubled her contribution to that cause because the recession had reduced this organization's income.

When I was director of development for the Boys and Girls Clubs of Chicago, a certain business executive told me, "I serve many boards because of my position. What you want is more of me for you, and less for them. You will have to earn more." We did. The man was heavily involved with us at the expense of his other organizations. We had measured up.

In conclusion, please note that the fall from commitment is a steep one. If commitment wavers for any reason, the chances of recovery are slim. We must always remember that we do not really motivate anybody. The best we can do is create an environment in which people motivate themselves.

Communication

> "I know you believe you understand what you think I said, but I'm not sure you realize that what you heard is not what I meant."
>
> —A quote from the author's niece

The problem of communication within a voluntary organization is complex. There are three primary communication issues which must be considered:

1. Interpersonal communications between individuals;
2. Interboard and intraboard communications;
3. Communications between the board and the public.

Nonprofit organizations must examine their procedures in all three of these areas. This chapter will not deal definitively with these issues because they are so broad; my purpose here is to bring them to the reader's attention.

Interpersonal communication between individuals

Unless the sender is extremely careful in the way he or she communicates, the impact of a message could be very different from the intent behind it. Written communications can always be misinterpreted. Spoken communications may be correct, but nonverbal communication can undercut what is spoken. Visuals, such as graphics, can convey one message; the

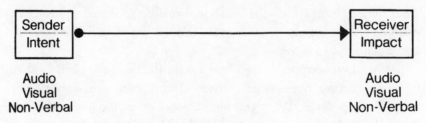

Figure 15–2. Message model

spoken word, another; and the nonverbal, a third. Cultural differences can also cause considerable difficulties—what is considered culturally correct by one person can be culturally anathema to another.

To complete the illustration of our message model, a feedback line must be added:

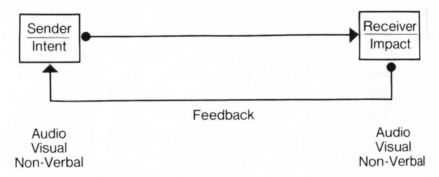

Figure 15-3. Message model with feedback

It is only through carefully constructed feedback processes that we can ensure that the impact of our message matches our intent. Much time is spent in the first phase of communication to the practical exclusion of the second, or feedback, phase. If more consideration were given to feedback, many communication problems could be eliminated.

Inter- and intraboard communications

A system of communication among board members—that is, intraboard—is imperative. In many organizations, so much time and effort is expended on communications between the board and the public that the *internal* mechanisms of communication are overlooked. It is important to have well-constructed board and committee meetings and concise, well-written communications (especially when it comes to meeting minutes and newsletters). There should be ample opportunity for small groups of board members to meet and work on specific tasks. Limited communications tend to narrow the decision-making process to a few people. The board can then become an oligarchy.

If the organization is a multi-unit one and the governing board has established unit boards to oversee the operations of the units, there may develop a different kind of communication problem, an interboard one. At the corporate level, it is very easy to make decisions that affect the local units without the participation of these units. The board of directors, of course, has the legal authority to make such decisions; but the exercise of this authority without consultation of the affected parties is of questionable wisdom.

Communications between the board and its publics

A board of directors has several publics: administration, administrative staff, line staff, and clients. The names given to these publics may vary among organizations, but the problem remains the same: If a board of directors is to have ultimate decision-making authority, how does it receive and interpret information necessary to making those decisions?

The chain-of-command system is efficient and swift. Information is filtered before reaching the board. Certain meetings can be dispensed with. This system, however, has two major problems. First, it gives the staff chief executive great power, for he or she is the main dispenser of information. What the board hears, essentially, is what the executive wants it to hear. Second, the board has little or no direct contact with its publics, which are represented through the administration. The whole effect is a very restricted perception of operations on the part of the board.

The open system has the decided advantage of open communications; everyone has direct access to the board. It also gives the board a much better perspective of what is going on in the organization. In addition, it affords the publics of the board an opportunity to participate in the process of the organization.

It has one major disadvantage, however. An enormous amount of time is required to implement such an open system. To maintain it requires longer meetings, in which everyone has the opportunity to speak. Moreover, individual board members can be the recipients of unlimited attempts at lobbying and endless complaints.

I prefer the system known as the open chain of command. It provides the best features of both the chain-of-command system and the open system. The board's publics can participate in the data-gathering process through participation on the various committees. This provides firsthand data for the board and great experience for the nonboard participants.

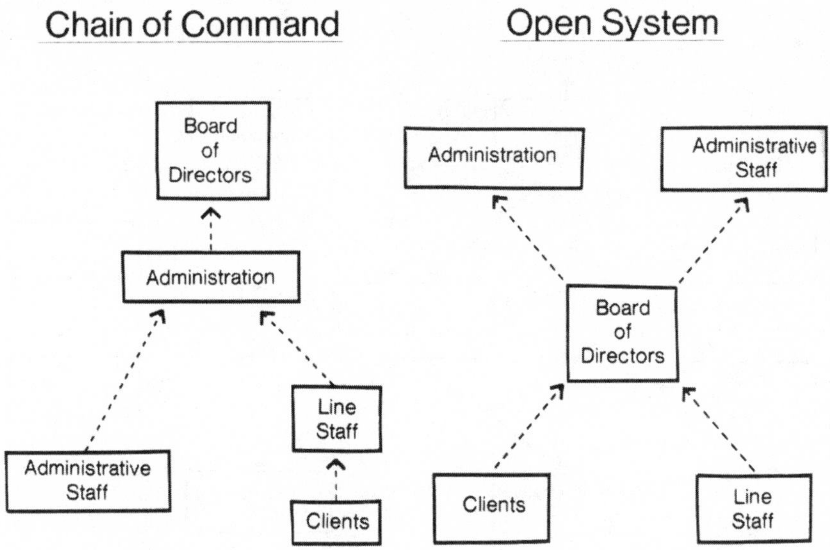

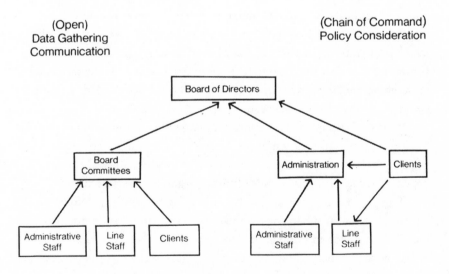

Chain of Command

Board of Directors

Administration

Administrative Staff

Line Staff

Clients

Open System

Administration

Administrative Staff

Board of Directors

Clients

Line Staff

Figure 15–4. Chain of command versus open system

(Open)
Data Gathering
Communication

(Chain of Command)
Policy Consideration

Board of Directors

Board Committees

Administration

Clients

Administrative Staff

Line Staff

Clients

Administrative Staff

Line Staff

Figure 15–5. Open chain of command

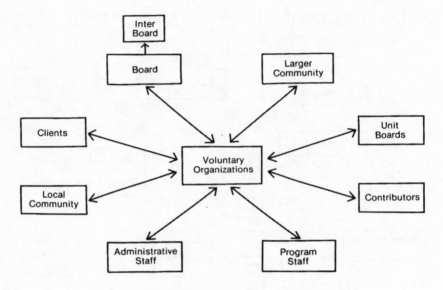

Figure 15-6. Communications network—organization and publics

Any requests for policy change or other decision-making should go through the chain of command. Administrative staff, line staff, and clients who wish to have issues heard by the board must go through the chain-of-command side. For this system to be effective, it should be made clear and understood by everyone. Any deviations should be avoided; exceptions will destroy the value of the system.

Figure 15-6 shows the voluntary organization at the center of the network—sending information to and receiving information from its publics. Figure 15-7 illustrates another network, one in which the publics communicate with each other, and the voluntary organization is excluded.

The significance of the side-by-side existence of these two networks becomes apparent when the voluntary organization sends out different messages to different publics, according to what it believes each particular public wishes to hear. The folly, of course, lies in the fact that the publics do talk among themselves. If one public finds out that it has received information different from that which was received by the other publics, organizational credibility is lost.

A final note on communication concerns information flow. Every staff member must understand and know the difference between the need-to-

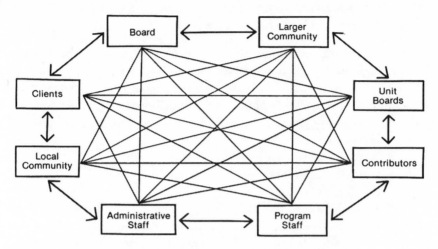

Figure 15–7. Communications network—publics only

know for decision-making, and the need-to-know for climate. The need-to-know for purposes of making a decision can be very narrow, usually restricted to a series of facts that lead to a logical conclusion. This type of need-to-know reduces the decision-making process to the level of mechanics. It likewise tends to constrict the thinking of those who have to make decisions to the tangible, the logical. The need-to-know for climate is more humanistic. This kind of data brings the decision-making process into more human terms and stirs the emotions of the recipient of the information, producing a sense of belonging and involvement.

Limiting the availability of information to the need-to-know for decision-making can cause organizations to become impersonal and result-oriented, at the expense of people. Information for climate, on the other hand, produces an environment more conducive to holistic thought.

The Board at Work

Knowledge without common sense is folly; without method, it is waste; without kindness, it is fanaticism; without religion, it is death. But with common sense, it is wisdom; with method, it is power; with charity, it is beneficence; with religion, it is virtue and life and peace.

—Anonymous

The following are a few issues relating to communications which must be addressed if the board is to function effectively and efficiently:

1. The board has a comprehensive strategic plan outlining where the organization ought to be in the future.
2. The board has an annual plan that is in harmony with the strategic plan.
3. The board does its planning before initiating the budget process.
4. There is adequate staff assistance for clerical work, data gathering, and so on.
5. Board members are generally accessible to staff.
6. Staff share relevant information with the board even though it may reflect negatively on staff work.
7. Board volunteers fulfill their commitments.
8. The board is willing to discuss and take action on controversial issues.
9. There is an adequate and definite process for data collection to facilitate board decision-making.
10. Board meetings reflect free and wide-ranging discussions, full participation, and respect for divergent opinions.
11. Board meetings generally focus on policy, review, evaluation, and reports of committees and task forces.
12. Members of the board or committee accept other board members and appreciate their strengths while understanding their weaknesses.
13. If board members find themselves in a minority position, they support the majority position as long as they remain a part of the board.
14. Routine matters are handled without time-wasting discussion.
15. Minutes of board and committee meetings are circulated to board members.
16. Reports of committee meetings are made to the board in a timely fashion.
17. The work of the committees is coordinated and monitored by the executive committee or board.
18. The board is composed of culturally diverse individuals who reflect the make-up of the community.
19. The board is composed of culturally diverse individuals who have been trained to work together.
20. Board members are able to communicate within the experience of others, giving full respect to others' values.
21. The board is adequately aware of ethnic and racial concerns.

22. How are differences and disagreements between board volunteers handled?
    a. Disagreements are usually ignored.
    b. Sometimes disagreements are accepted and worked through, sometimes they are ignored.
    c. Disagreements are usually accepted as necessary and desirable and worked through.
23. How are disagreements between staff and board members handled?
    a. Disagreements are usually ignored.
    b. Sometimes disagreements are accepted and worked through, sometimes they are ignored.
    c. Disagreements are usually accepted as necessary and desirable and worked through.
24. Board members are aware of and accept board functions.
25. Board members are aware of and accept board member roles.
26. Board members are aware of and accept staff functions.
27. Board members are aware of and accept staff roles.
28. Individual board members do not attempt to represent the board outside of board meetings without board sanction.
29. The board considers issues on the local, state, regional, and national levels within the organization's purpose.
30. Board members support staff if they are unjustly criticized.
31. The board conducts an annual review of its own work.
32. The board collaborates with other agencies in the community and is familiar with their programs and activities.
33. The board schedules its own continuing education programs, including at least one meeting annually without the pressures of a formal board or committee business meeting.

Today we all realize that boards of directors are not a self-perpetuating virus adapted to any body politic—that was the assumption of a previous generation. Boards of directors, we now know, are a special type of organism requiring specific nutriment materials—some economic, some social and cultural.

16

The Board Meeting

A board of directors exists or has legal status only when it meets. When it does meet, it has legal status only when the requirements for board volunteer attendance (quorum), board action (voting), and prior notice of meeting are met, as stipulated in the bylaws. The only deviations from this rule are those occasions when the board may vote on an issue through unanimous consent. This means the board can vote while not in session, as long as the vote is unanimous and each member signs a unanimous consent form.

Board meetings have an unfortunate tendency to become ritualistic and trivial. A common example of ritualistic board actions is the automatic approval of staff or committee reports with little or no discussion and no understanding of the issues involved or their impact on the organization. By trivial, I mean discussion that focuses on a minor policy or on administrative items rather than on larger issues that affect the organization. Hours can be spent discussing what color to paint the rooms, while the issue of accumulating deficits goes unattended.

When board meetings become ritualistic and trivial, a board is beginning to abandon its legal and ethical responsibilities. A board can delegate authority and responsibility, but it can never delegate or abdicate the final accountability for its actions. Furthermore, the actions of a board of directors also carry ethical implications. Decisions are not made in a vacuum: Each decision has an impact on clients, staff, and community

Trivial and ritualistic board meetings not only have serious legal and ethical implications, but they are also destructive of board member participation. Such meetings are superficial, and constitute an inexcusable waste of talent and other resources. Board meetings should be the focal point of organization action. Committee meetings, staff meetings, and community meetings are designed to support the board in its deliberations.

Remember, a board of directors has four basic functions:

1. Determine the Work to Be Done;
2. Within the Work to Be Done, decide policy and who is to be held accountable for implementation;
3. Implement specified policy;
4. Monitor and evaluate policy decisions.

The primary purpose of the board meeting is to address these functions. There are, however, secondary purposes, by-products, or conditions necessary for effective board meetings that are not themselves primary purposes. A board meeting is not a social event or a place to get to know one another— although sociability may be a by-product or may be important to success. It is not an educational meeting. Although board meetings can be educational, the real education takes place outside of the board meeting. Although information and communication are integral to a good board meeting, it is not the function of the board to hold meetings that are merely informational. And although inspiration is often a factor, it is not the sole aim of a board meeting. Board meetings must focus on their primary functions, that is, policy making and policy monitoring. The four by-products or conditions for successful meetings must be planned for separately. The board must ask itself:

1. How do we provide for sociability?
2. How do we provide for education?
3. How do we provide for information/communication?
4. Do we inspire?

To fail to answer these questions is to detract form the conditions necessary to carry out the essential functions of the board meeting.

There is a policy and monitoring cycle in the board meeting, as illustrated in Figure 16–1. Most policy decisions are made at the end of the

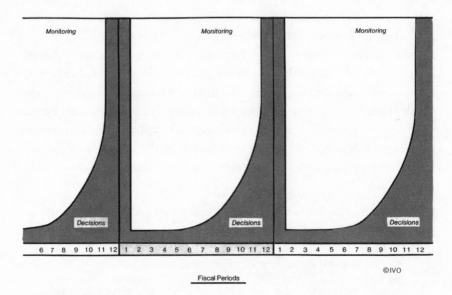

Monitoring   Monitoring   Monitoring

Decisions   Decisions   Decisions

6 7 8 9 10 11 12 | 1 2 3 4 5 6 7 8 9 10 11 12 | 1 2 3 4 5 6 7 8 9 10 11 12

©IVO

Fiscal Periods

Figure 16–1. Board of directors policy cycle

current year to be implemented in the following year. The first month of the fiscal period is used primarily to modify previous decisions. Fiscal months two through ten are primarily reserved for monitoring, with decisions escalating to the eleventh and twelfth months.

Board-Committee Meeting Cycle

Voluntary organizations often have too many board meetings. It is important to keep in mind the cycle illustrated in Figure 16–2. As a rule of thumb, if there are effective committee and executive committee meetings going on, board meetings need occur only four to six times a year, with quarterly meetings the minimum. Board meeting agendas flow from the work of committees and from current operating issues. Good board meetings, therefore, require good committee meetings. As in committee meetings, the agenda and related data should be mailed out in advance of the board meeting.

One of the problems of board and committee meetings is that assignments are made and accepted, then buried in minutes and forgotten. Figure 16–3 shows an easy way to keep track of issue flow and assignments. This

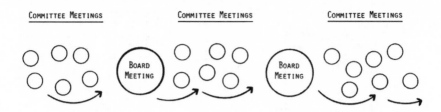

COMMITTEE MEETINGS   COMMITTEE MEETINGS   COMMITTEE MEETINGS

BOARD MEETING   BOARD MEETING

Figure 16-2. Board-committee meeting cycle

chart can be used for board, committee, and staff meetings. The chair and staff member should each have copies to revise and make assignments.

A good board meeting can be a strong motivator. A bad board meeting —or a series of them—is deadly. With regard to newly recruited board members, it is important to remember that this is their first look at the organization. Organizations cannot afford to have that first look tarnished. One good method of keeping board meetings focused and on-point is to have a calendar, as illustrated in Figure 16-4.

NEWPORT ORGANIZATION

Board of Directors	ISSUE FLOW AND ASSIGNMENT				
Organizational Component					Date

ISSUE	SOURCE	ASSIGNMENT	REPORTING PERSON	DUE DATE	ACTION REQUIRED
Poor handling of switch board	Public complaint	Staff Executive Director	Bob Johnson	--------	Resolve problem
No policy for use of bequests	Budget Committee	Business Committee	Tom Clark	May Board Meeting	Policy decision
Moisture entering west wing of bldg.	Staff to Building Committee	Property Committee to get bids	Joe Block	May Board Meeting	Decision on contract letting
Accounting proposal	Staff	Business Committee	Tom Clark	June Board Meeting	Policy decision
Interior painting schedule with costs	Board member	Property Comm. in consultation with Business Committee	Joe Block	Aug. Board Meeting	Approval to submit to Finance Committee
Issue 6	Property Committee	Business Committee	Tom Clark	Oct. Board Meeting	Decision for expenditure
Request for individual tutoring	Parents to staff	Program Committee	Juanita Perez	Oct. Board Meeting	Board approval
Report progress on Teen Center	Board member	Program Committee	Herman Dent	Nov. Board Meeting	Information only

Figure 16-3. Issue flow and assignment

NEWPORT ORGANIZATION

BOARD CALENDAR FOR 20_

MONTH	TASK	DATE
January or Fiscal Month #1	1. Budgets finalized for current year.	Jan. 7
	2. City-Wide meetings of Unit standing committee chairmen with corresponding Corporate committee chairmen.	Jan. 15
	3. Annual meeting	Jan. 20
February or Fiscal Month #2	1. General campaign kick-off.	Feb. 1
	2. General Report Meeting.	Feb. 15
	3. Boards of Managers Report Meeting.	Feb. 25
	4. Board of Directors Report Meeting.	Feb. 28
March or Fiscal Month #3	1. General Report Meeting.	March 4
	2. Boards of Managers Report Meeting.	March 15
	3. Budget preparation kits distributed.	March 25
	4. Board of Directors Report Meeting.	March 28
	5. Executive Committee Meeting.	March 31
April or Fiscal Month #4	1. General Report Meeting.	April 5
	2. Boards of Managers Report Managers.	April 15
	3. Building inspection by Boards of Managers Property Committee.	April 20
	4. Preparation of budgets.	April 25
	5. Board of Directors Report Meeting.	April 28
	6. Board Meeting.	April 30
May or Fiscal Month #5	1. Final General Report Meeting.	May 5
	2. Boards of Managers Report Meeting.	May 14
	3. Budget process continues.	May 20
	4. Building inspection continued.	May 22
	5. Board of Directors Report Meeting.	May 30
June or Fiscal Month #6	1. Unit and Camp budgets approved by Boards of Managers and submitted to the Associate Executive Director.	June 6
	2. Executive Committee Meeting.	June 28
July or Fiscal Month #7	1. Budgets reviewed by Corporate Program Services Committee.	July 10
	2. Board Meeting.	July 25
August or Fiscal Month #8	1. Budgets reviewed by Corporate Reviewing Committee.	Aug. 10
September or Fiscal Month #9	1. Preliminary budget approval.	Sept. 15
	2. Financial Development Committees appoint Campaign Chairmen.	Sept. 20
	3. Nominating Committees elected.	Sept. 25
	4. Executive Committee Meeting.	Sept. 30
October or Fiscal Month #10	1. City-Wide planning meeting of all campaign chairmen.	Oct. 1
	2. Campaign chairmen recruit Corporate Division chairmen and Community Division chairmen.	Oct. 5
	3. Selection of team captains by campaign chairmen and division chairmen.	Oct. 15
	4. Board Meeting.	Oct. 20
November or Fiscal Month #11	1. Election of officers.	Nov. 8
	2. Divisional chairmen recruit team captains.	Nov. 15
December or Fiscal Month #12	1. Appointment of standing committee chairmen.	Dec. 10
	2. Meeting of team captains.	Dec. 15
	3. Executive Committee Meeting.	Dec. 18

Figure 16–4. Board calendar

Building a Board Meeting Agenda

Reports concerning the program of the organization (e.g., program services committee, executive director) should be first on the agenda. These items will set the tone for the balance of the meeting. Don't allow the meeting to become bogged down in items that are essentially maintenance as opposed to movement. Maintenance items can be printed up and mailed out in advance of the meeting. Little time needs to be spent on these.

Aside from the reports of the executive director, all reports should be made by board members. Board meetings are for board members; they are not staff meetings. Staff who have committee assignments should sit with their committee chair, but should play no role unless asked specific questions. If ad hoc committees or task forces have been appointed, they should have a place on the agenda for a report.

CONCEPTS:

1. Board meetings should largely reflect work of committees.

2. The Board of Directors takes action on committee recommendation, thereby creating policy.

3. New and old business appear under committee reports.

COMMITTEE MEETINGS

Executive . . . .

Program Services . . . .

Resource Development . . . .

    Membership . . . .

    Planned Giving . . . .

    Public Relations . . . .

    Campaign . . . .

Finance . . . .

    Budget . . . .

    Property . . . .

Human Resources . . . .

NEWPORT ORGANIZATION
BOARD OF DIRECTORS MEETING

April 28, 20__

AGENDA

Elliot P. Sampson, Chairperson
Presiding

1. Approval of Agenda--1 minute

2. Approval of Minutes--3 minutes
                      Mr. Cannon, Secretary
3. Executive Director's Report--10 minutes
                      Mr. Klein
4. Executive Committee Report--2 minutes
                      Mr. Sampson
5. Program Services Committee Report--10 minutes
                      Mrs. Perez

6. Resource Development Committee Report
   a. Membership--5 minutes   Mr. Hogan
   b. Planned Giving--5 minutes   Mr. Cobb
   c. Public Relations--5 minutes   Mr. Sanchez
   d. Campaign--10 minutes   Mr. Shortz

7. Finance Committee Report   Mr. Pierce
   a. Budget--10 minutes   Mr. Jenner
   b. Property--10 minutes   Ms. Lyttle

8. Human Resources--5 minutes   Mr. Pratt

9. Chair's Report--5 minutes   Mr. Sampson

10. Adjournment

Figure 16–5. Building a board meeting agenda

For a more complete discussion of this topic, the following two monographs may be useful:

Board and Committee Meetings
Do Your Board Meetings Motivate or Turn Off?

See our website for information on how to order: www.ifvo.org.

Many times I attend a board meeting to observe how the meeting is conducted and to evaluate the agenda and its effectiveness. There is a simple, three-part template that I apply to the meeting that will provide useful information about the board/staff relationship. As I observe the conduct of those in the meeting, their behavior usually falls into one of the following three categories:

1. The staff give most of the reports and dominate the meeting.
2. Board members make reports. However, the reports are handed to the board members when they enter the room and the staff handle the questions that arise from the report.
3. The board members come into the meeting bringing their own reports, which they have worked on with the assistance of the staff in advance of the meeting. When questions about the report arise, the board members handle most of the questions.

Three is best. Where do your board meetings fit?

17

Staff Attitudes toward Boards

The following are twenty-three questions designed to establish a pattern of beliefs about boards. These beliefs affect staff attitudes. Attitudes in turn affect behavior. Staff must be aware of their beliefs about boards. If a staff member has a low score, perhaps he or she should examine his or her belief system about boards. Boards can easily detect a staff's attitude toward boards by their behavior—or lack of behavior.

Questions

1. Volunteers are very important to a nonprofit organization.
   AGREE_____ NOT SURE _____ DISAGREE_____

2. I believe that people will give freely of their time and resources to nonprofit organizations.
   AGREE _____ NOT SURE _____ DISAGREE_____

3. I find it satisfying and productive to work with a board of directors.
   AGREE _____ NOT SURE _____ DISAGREE _____

4. I believe that a well trained and informed board of directors can make the right decisions which affect the nonprofit organization.
   AGREE _____ NOT SURE _____ DISAGREE _____

5. I am comfortable with the role of "enabler" with a board of directors. Enabler means the staff provide all support required to "enable" the board to be successful in its function.
   AGREE _____ NOT SURE _____ DISAGREE _____

6. I can deal with a board of directors truthfully at all times.
   AGREE _____ NOT SURE _____ DISAGREE _____

7. I can trust a board of directors to honor the confidentiality of certain information it possesses.
   AGREE _____ NOT SURE _____ DISAGREE _____

8. I believe that most boards can rise above personal and factional concerns to deal with organizational issues on an objective basis.
   AGREE _____ NOT SURE _____ DISAGREE _____

9. I find it difficult to believe that people join boards to help rather than to take over.
   AGREE _____ NOT SURE _____ DISAGREE _____

10. If the board decides against staff recommendations, I can wholeheartedly implement the decisions even though it is contrary to my belief.
    AGREE _____ NOT SURE _____ DISAGREE _____

11. I believe that most board members will follow through on commitments.
    AGREE _____ NOT SURE _____ DISAGREE _____

12. Boards of directors can and will take initiatives and be creative within their assigned roles.
    AGREE _____ NOT SURE _____ DISAGREE _____

13. I prepare agendas for board and committee meetings, as the board members have little need to be concerned with agendas.
    AGREE _____ NOT SURE _____ DISAGREE _____

14. Board members are free to give advice to and seek information from staff.
    AGREE _____ NOT SURE _____ DISAGREE _____

15. Each board member has the responsibility to represent the organization and to serve as advocate in the community.
    AGREE _____ NOT SURE _____ DISAGREE _____

16. It is my decision what information is to go before the board.
    AGREE _____ NOT SURE _____ DISAGREE _____

17. I should rely on only a few board volunteers for decisions, especially the ones who know me well and agree with the organization's direction.
    AGREE _____ NOT SURE _____ DISAGREE _____

18. I rarely discuss controversial issues with the board or put those on agendas.
    AGREE _____ NOT SURE _____ DISAGREE _____

19. In a sense, the board only ratifies staff decisions.
    AGREE _____ NOT SURE _____ DISAGREE _____

20. My organization would run just as well if the board were in an advisory status.
    AGREE _____ NOT SURE _____ DISAGREE _____

21. My organization's credibility in the community depends upon the board.
    AGREE _____ NOT SURE _____ DISAGREE _____

22. My board volunteers are laypersons with little or no <u>professional</u> skill and insight that is appropriate for this organization.
    AGREE _____ NOT SURE _____ DISAGREE _____

23. Mainly because I'm full time, I am in a better position than the board to discover and evaluate the community's interest and needs.
    AGREE _____ NOT SURE _____ DISAGREE _____

Scoring

Questions: Circle your score for each question.

	Agree	Not Sure	Disagree
1.	2	1	0
2.	2	1	0
3.	2	1	0
4.	2	1	0
5.	2	1	0
6.	2	1	0
7.	2	1	0
8.	2	1	0
9.	0	1	2

10.	2	1	0
11.	2	1	0
12.	2	1	0
13.	0	1	2
14.	2	1	0
15.	2	1	0
16.	0	1	2
17.	0	1	2
18.	0	1	2
19.	0	1	2
20.	0	1	2
21.	2	1	0
22.	0	1	2
23.	0	1	2

Total the scores within your circled score. Less than a perfect score of 46 suggests that the respondent should examine his or her attitudes with regard to those issues or scoring zero points. Answers to these questions are found throughout this book.

You can contact Bill Conrad at e-mail billconrad2@attbi.com, at (630) 964-0432, or through our website: www.ifvo.org. to discuss your questions.

For the board member counterpart to this test, order *My Perceptions of Boards—A Self-Discovery Process* from the Voluntary Management Press at www.ifvo.org or (630) 964-0432.

Section VI

What Can Go Wrong and How to Fix It

18

Enabling Technology

In the past decade there has been a quantum leap in the information available to nonprofits. Matching this increase is the technology available to access, process, and organize this information. Nonprofits today must plan carefully for the use of technology.

The following is by Deborah Strauss, Executive Director, and Tim Mills-Groninger, Associate Executive Director, of the IT Resource Center.

The IT Resource Center is a nonprofit organization dedicated to helping nonprofits effectively utilize computers and other technology.

The IT Resource Center is sixteen years old. Its core programs include basic information about computers, orientation sessions that focus on common computer applications, planning sessions to assist in analyzing computer requirements, making purchase decisions and troubleshooting. Hands on training is offered in word processing, spreadsheet, database, desktop publishing, the Internet, operating systems and other subjects.

Special projects include CompuMentor/Chicago, which matches computer professionals with organizations requesting specific assistance.

IT Resource Center sponsors NPO, NET, which is an information service for the Chicago area nonprofit community.

For further information about the IT Resource Center:

6 N. Michigan Ave.
Suite 1405
Chicago, IL 60602
Phone: 312–372–4872
Fax: 312–372–7962
Website: www.npo.net/itrc

No one would argue that having the right information at the right time and for the right price is one of the keys to effectively managing any organization. For nonprofit organizations in particular, reliable information is critical to determining the need for services, to planning delivery mechanisms, and to evaluating outcomes. The challenge is to manage information creatively and effectively. Information should advance the needs of customers, whether the definition of customer is the population served, the donors and funders who provide the wherewithal to provide those services, or internal management.

Technology can be the driving force in this process. It is a generally accepted fact that work assisted by automation is done more quickly and more accurately. At the same time, information is thought of as an administrative chore, rarely, if ever, as a corporate asset. Organizations that have committed to the integration of information management into their overall infrastructure tend to be above average in terms of accountability. Consequently, they tend to become the survivors in terms of funding.

The organizations presented in these case studies are composites seen in the IT Resource Center's fifteen-year history of work with 1,300 Chicago-area organizations. While some situations may seem apocryphal, each has been observed at least once, and many numerous times. We show that even the most successful planning endeavor involves mistakes and missteps. By chronicling the process, warts and all, we hope that you will recognize circumstances relevant to your own organization. While the organizations presented are not meant to be identifiable, the circumstances are—particularly the fabric of personality, organizational structure, and how challenges are met. Not every decision was correct, and even the best planning process involves missteps and pitfalls. If you recognize yourself in any situation, you are not alone.

Technology Planning—New Opportunities for Problem Solving

When we talk about information management, we are placing a greater emphasis on the content—the information, and its role in decision making, than on the tools—the computer systems and other technologies employed. Post-it notes and legal pads are as much a part of an organizational information system as a file server or report generator. That's not to say that hardware and software is not important, but rather that their selection and use should meet business needs—they must truly provide leverage, and not just be fashionable.

Technology can be used in two ways: to solve a problem or to provide an opportunity for major reorganization of how work is done. The first, problem solving, tends to be how computing machinery has been customarily employed.

The second, using technology to make new work possible (referred to as enabling technology in books on business and codependency), can radically change how an organization functions. These changes come from working outward from mission to the programs that support it. Both automated and manual procedures that are maintained out of habit should be examined in terms of their contribution to the mission goals. New processes that can advance program goals should be explored. A procedure's overall efficiency in terms of technological opportunities or best business practices should be the criteria for retention, reengineering, or elimination.

System Development Issues

In our first two case studies, we will show successful approaches to planning, implementation, and management. The first case shows how senior management's adherence to a conventional management structure coupled with corporate disinterest in the details of information technology provide an opportunity for a strong MIS director to advance the strategic goals of the agency because it was the right thing to do. This was clearly an instance where the right people, given the right incentive (in this case, benign neglect) did the right thing.

The second case study shows the more common situation where there never was a plan; the information system evolved as a reaction to a series of short-term crises. In this case the re-engineering of the organization coincided with a low point in user confidence in the support structure. A team representing a wide base of user interests was able to organize and sustain a critical evaluation of the status quo with the sanction of the executive committee.

Case Study Number 1:
Two Generations of Planning

Our first case study is about an organization that took the traditional problem-solving approach in its first generation data processing system, but gradually moved to a more aggressive use of information technology to advance agency goals.

The local chapter of a national human service organization was an early adopter of computer technology for all of the traditional reasons: They were big, with over one hundred employees, and they had lots of paper to manage. Fund raising involved millions of dollars from hundreds of thousands of donors, both corporate and individual, and there were accounting, human resource, and other administrative chores that private industry had already automated.

At the time, large computers required a large capital investment and a significant commitment to operations. The traditional installation had a centralized management structure, and information itself was closely held. Information was often distributed as printed reports, making any kind of comprehensive evaluation of trends a lengthy and tedious process.

It made perfect sense to computerize by the late 1970s, after a cost benefit analysis conducted by a big-eight accounting firm found that computerization paid for itself within five years and would save money from that point forward. The national organization provided little direct support or supervision, so it was up to the chapter to blaze its own trail. The conservative and highly corporate board of directors did the conservative and highly corporate thing, which was to use the information management model then in vogue.

The Corporate Management Model

Based on a second study produced by the accounting firm (discounted, but not pro-bono) the board created a new department for management information systems and set out to create an automated data processing system.

Because the board mandate had been to save money and solve obvious problems, not look for trouble, the newly hired MIS director believed there was no need to rush things. Over a period of almost two years, internal requirements were assembled from direct observation and user interviews; simultaneously, these requirements were compared to those of other chapters around the country and to the corporations represented on the board. As solutions were identified in other organizations, the MIS staff would produce thumbnail sketches of the staffing, hardware, software, and other system components employed. After several such benchmarking exercises, a certain pattern emerged (remember this was the late seventies).

Not surprisingly, the MIS staff found that most successful systems were staffed by full-time professionals who were paid the prevailing wage. The most common hardware and software combination was a proprietary minicomputer with a mix of off-the-shelf and slightly customized applications. Information management was centrally controlled, and MIS would meet the information access needs of the rest of the staff with deference and courtesy, if not without the occasionally condescending smile.

Management vs. Staff

By the late 1980s the world had changed. Database management systems had shifted from centralized control to distributed systems. The minicomputer as well as the central computer that everyone went to for data, was being replaced by a desktop system capable of storing and processing huge amounts of data according to the needs and preferences of a single user. This shift provided the opportunity for the Chapter to change how services were managed, delivered, and evaluated. While the system was functioning well within its design specifications, those specifications were nearly ten years old, as was the hardware. The corporate culture had also changed. Where once outside studies were almost mandatory before making a major decision, now every expense had to be justified. Where ample staffing had been seen as insurance, now headcounts adversely affected overhead. Where the board had been composed of captains of industry whose good corporate citizenship was synonymous with largess, the same individuals now represented downsizing and return on investment. Capital improvements to the computer system were not a priority item.

What's an MIS director to do? The traditional approach would be corporate musical chairs: as the environment changed, staff uncomfortable or threatened in the new environment would leave to take similar positions in other companies. Their replacements would make changes based on personal preference and priorities established during the job interview, and when the terrain shifted again, they would move to another position. This is what headhunters live for, and it can produce short-term benefits. Lots of changes will eventually get something right.

The Chapter's MIS director took a much longer view. While organizational and technological changes had undermined user confidence and management's belief in the system's continued cost effectiveness, the MIS director tried to convert that concern into a reasonable justification for a system review. The first time the argument was presented, it failed because senior management took the position that no working administrative systems or policies would be changed. The MIS director was, for the time being, stuck with the problem of being too successful in the original system construction.

Opportunities for Change

The system chugged along managing donor lists, accounting, service statistics, and other large-scale functions while microcomputers were brought in here and there as a part of departmental budgets to solve smaller problems. MIS staff added microcomputer support to their suite of skills, and two independent systems began to emerge. It was not until the board announced a move of the Chapter's offices to less expensive space that the MIS director saw the opportunity to consolidate the divergent systems. Where senior management saw the move as a simple cost-cutting measure aimed at reducing overhead, the MIS director saw it as a chance to redesign the way information flowed in the agency.

While the MIS department had originally been conceived as a hedge against repetitive work and a means to faster processing of data, the MIS director had built a department very well focused on meeting user demand for information in whatever form necessary. Not that MIS staff completely abandoned their minicomputer backgrounds; the first response to the move was to develop a cabling plan that would accommodate the existing minicomputer terminals *and* a PC-based Local Area Network. The justification was to preserve as much of the existing system as possible, but allow for the inclusion of PCs later on.

Over time the MIS director developed a strategic plan that balanced the need to distribute the responsibility for data (input, processing, and evaluation) to the desktop level with the need to maintain data integrity. Centralized data structures may have frustrated staff with their rigidity, but data were always consistent, and backups were done every day by MIS staff. Giving staff information cooked to order was quite a challenge. Over time, it translated into a hierarchical policy in which anyone on staff could have access to information, fewer people could have authority to add or change data (and then only when they confirmed to established procedures), and fewer still could change the structure of the system, (and then only after a comprehensive review process). The core database and accounting systems remained centralized on the recently upgraded minicomputer. Processes that were not critical to the database were moved to stand-alone PCs and to a small LAN. As expertise with the LAN increased, more users were moved to it. Later, access to the minicomputer from the LAN was added.

Corporate downsizing played its own role as well. While the number of MIS staff decreased through attrition and a hiring freeze, the number of users of the system increased. A small part of this change can be attributed to the overstaffing of the department when it was originally formed, but even more can be attributed to the changes in the environment. When the system was entirely minicomputer based, MIS staff had to train and support all users on the database and proprietary word-processing software. The word-processing software could best be described as archaic, and even simple merges and reports could be a nightmare. But with the shift from the minicomputer to PCs and generic word-processing software, training was readily available on the open market, and users were much more willing to learn skills that they felt were valuable. MIS support activities correspondingly shifted from the direct and time-consuming task of end user support to the background role of maintaining the infrastructure.

MIS as Asset

Politically, this shift left MIS in the unenviable position of being largely invisible—as long as things worked. When things went wrong, and they always do, the user community would be up in arms over any delays in response. But the effort to keep the system running was widely ignored. The MIS director, having brought the department into the agency and transformed it from a back-office data processing shop to a user assistance and support center, now set out to make the final shift to positioning MIS as a strategic asset. The case was made to senior management and to the board of governors that the information now held in the various donor databases could be used much more aggressively, and the information now available on the desktop level could be used much more creatively. Likewise, the shortened production cycles of word-processing documents, now using a widely accepted word-processing program that required less MIS involvement in support, had made much of the MIS department's downsizing possible.

Where agency wide staff and budget cuts had been somewhat random in the first round of downsizing, MIS now had an assortment of tools to assist the remaining staff to advance agency mission while meeting mandates to do more with less. The board bought technology as a way to make downsizing work, but only on a limited basis. While staff had access to information and could evaluate different programs and activities, there was not a corresponding shift in control. The board still liked a centralized reporting structure, and employee empowerment was defined as going through channels. Staff had much greater access to data, but the freedom to use and manipulate information to new purposes required authorization. The smaller organizational structure made the approval process more efficient and few requests for database enhances were denied. An unexpected benefit of the policy was that more people knew about changes, and often found unanticipated uses in their own areas.

The key success factors in this system remain: Developing a department responsive to agency goals and user needs, even when there was not a clear mandate to do so. Developing as flexible an approach as possible given the environment (the board's tendencies towards using the current corporate models) and available technologies (minicomputers in the early '80s, LANs in the early '90s). It was an opportunistic approach to change: do a good job, avoid crisis, and wait for the right moment to advance a new plan.

Case Study #2: The Battered User Syndrome

Sometimes it's hard to manage the process because there was never a plan for automation, just a gradual infiltration of technology. Computers found their way into the Council, a national social service coordinating agency, by happenstance. With about fifty staff and a history of legislative advocacy and technical assistance for service planning for health care providers, data processing had not played a big role in the first thirty years of the Council's existence.

Major decision-making came from an executive committee composed of division heads. The board was not part of day-to-day operations and would generally agree to any recommendations from the committee. The culture of the organization had evolved over the years until each division was a fairly autonomous unit with its own management style, budget, and organizational structure.

Hardware Purchase As Solution

Microcomputers were purchased on a case-by-case basis, usually at the insistence of the person who would be using the system. Over the period of several years a heterogeneous environment emerged: the marketing and membership Division used Macs for desktop publishing and a simple flat-file database to track media contacts and local affiliates. The development office had been early adopters of a non-programmable relational database to track corporate and individual gifts, and the program evaluation division had moved from terminals connected to a university mainframe to high-powered desktop PCs for statistical analyses. Each new project brought a new project director with a particular hardware and software preference. Computers appeared on desktops like mushrooms after a rainstorm.

Concealing Real Problems with Technology

Corporate culture encouraged hardware purchases because hardware could be touched and seen—a machine sitting on a desk proved that something had been done. Application software was regarded much differently: the executive committee did not interact with software directly. All they ever saw were the results—which for the reports and proposals that crossed their desks did not look all that different from what they had been seeing all their lives. Consequently, an attitude developed that training and technical support needs were a sign of weakness. Any person who knew how to do his or her job should know how to use a computer automatically.

Technical Support through Folklore and the Oral Tradition

Over time a subculture of underground training and peer support emerged. Staff members would never publicly admit that they did not know how to do something, but they would privately seek out an unofficial guru, either on staff or through personal contacts, to get the help they needed. When a local technical college offered to place a team of students in the office as part of a class project, the Council's executive committee readily agreed. For sixteen weeks the team focused on basic configuration and support issues. Much of the time was spent optimizing systems and figuring out components, such as print sharing devices that had been purchased but never installed. Soon the team was completely integrated into the Council's everyday life—if someone needed a file converted from one of the MS-DOS machines to the Macs, the task would wait until a team member appeared. When it was time to change the toner cartridge, one of the team members would do it. The development office relinquished responsibility for designing and maintaining the database to the students. Staff liked having the additional support and told the executive committee that they could not be as productive without it.

After the class project was completed, the Council hired two of the students, Marvin and Troy, to provide ongoing support on a part-time basis. Within two years, their billing increased until the Council was paying close to $50,000 annually for support and maintenance charges.

In short order staff became captive to the peculiarities of the consultants. For instance, their approach to databases was to have one list for each activity (board, affiliates, community groups, donors) and manually synchronize changes where the lists overlapped (a number of donors were with community groups or affiliate agencies). Address changes in particular could take days to complete, and over time, staff became fearful of using the system and invoking Troy's wrath for using something that was not ready. Staff could do data entry and simple queries, but any substantive work waited until the days Troy was in and felt like doing them. A more qualified consultant would have centralized addresses into a single mailing list and used the advantages of relational software to track additional information.

Blame Seeking

Staff's increasing dependency on the consultants grew, and Marvin in particular changed from a technical support resource to a technology tyrant. He had very strong opinions about the right way to do things and what software to use. Marvin's disdain for staff grew as systems became more complex and personally challenging for him while requests for support remained simple and uninteresting.

Building a Planning Team

And so things remained until the executive committee started a strategic planning process. Information management, while not on any of the original agendas, soon became a major concern. Marvin and Troy's approach to strategic planning had been simply to create lists of new equipment to purchase and enhancements to the databases. The executive committee liked the idea of more hardware, but staff was livid at the idea of more of the same. Several staff were extremely concerned that relying on an occasionally surly and always uncommunicative vendor for technical support was not in the agency's best interests. Several staff lobbied heavily for a needs-driven approach to information management, instead of the traditional hardware approach.

An early result of strategic planning was a recognition that the existing practice of autonomous divisions was redundant and inefficient. One of the action steps to improve interdivision cooperation was to form interdisciplinary teams to work on specific projects or problems. The project team approach worked; people were talking to each other more easily, and expertise was available where it was needed.

A small cadre of staff saw an opportunity in the team concept and hatched a plan. One of the preset limits of strategic planning was that staff size would not increase, nor would any new divisions be created. Understanding that no full-time computer support staff were possible, let alone the creation of an MIS division, the group petitioned for the creation of a computer committee. The executive committee, delighted at a show of initiative that was consistent with the strategic plan and would not cost anything but time, approved.

The consultants viewed the planning process as unrelated to their goals and the creation of the computer committee as a kind of user group that further relieved them of day-to-day support functions. The committee saw its role as facilitating the free flow of information between divisions in order to make the project teams effective. Their first order of business was to address the deficiencies in computer support, which was where the ITRC became involved, first as consultants, and then as trainers.

Authority

The initial desire was to have every staff member able to provide his or her own support, in effect making everyone super-users. Our recommendation was to take a multi-tiered approach and designate a Computer Responsible

Person or CRP for each workgroup. The CRP (often pronounced "creep") concept serves a number of purposes. First, it gives a name to the job function that permits a fairly wide latitude in job description. The primary function of CRPs is to know what they don't know about the system, and where to go for help. Even relative computer neophytes can be CRPs if they are willing to learn what the system is supposed to do and who to call when it stops. CRPs can solve problems by themselves, or they can call in reinforcements according to a preset policy—it does not matter as long as they can resolve the problem. The Council's computer committee decided that its members would become CRPs and so took responsibility not only for making recommendations for system improvements, but for making them happen as well.

To us, as outside observers, the situation was fairly clear: The original consultants were not responsive to user needs and were, through a display of passive/aggressive behavior, fighting the change in organizational focus. The CRPs saw it differently; in almost every early meeting someone would begin an exchange along the lines of: "Troy will throw a fit if you try that." "Well, let's fire Troy, and Marvin as well, and use their contract money to do it right." "Then who would run my month ending reports? I don't have time to learn how to do it myself. . . ." The CRPs, like so many battered spouses, wanted to take control of the situation, but were afraid that they would not be able to provide for themselves if they did. Troy was the only link into the confusing web of databases, and Marvin was providing the maintenance contract for all of the hardware.

Things were at an impasse until the CRPs decided that, in order to make it on their own, they would need more direct experience in how the systems work and thus created a CRP boot camp. For two weeks one set of CRPs did little more than take covers off machines, peer inside laser printers, and document configuration files. The remaining CRPs engaged in what we call "digital archeology," the art of divining the purpose and uses of database systems without benefit of documentation or designer. At the end of the process, the CRPs felt that they could live and prosper in the age AM&T (After Marvin and Troy).

Confidence was high, and the CRPs proposed sweeping changes to the executive committee. They wanted to terminate the maintenance and support contract with Marvin and Troy when it came up for renewal at the end of the quarter. The money saved would be put into hardware purchases to replace the most ancient hardware and into additional staff training on the systems already in place. Likewise they proposed a centralized Development and Marketing and Membership database. In the next budget cycle they would argue for consolidation of the disparate networks and additional system improvements.

There was significant risk in this plan. In order for it to work, no money was allocated for repair for the remainder of the fiscal year—if any hardware failed, there would be a scramble to find the money to repair it. There was some concern also that Troy had build traps into the database that could cause a catastrophic data loss. Some were worried that Marvin, who had previously had no compunction about installing unlicensed software all over the office, might turn them in to the authorities for software piracy.

Considerable thought went into the contract termination. Marvin and Troy were informed three weeks before the end of the quarter that the contract would not be renewed. They rapidly went through the stages of anger, denial, negotiation, and, finally, acceptance. The remaining time on the current contract was to go into an extensive debrief of how they did their jobs to aid the CRPs in formalizing policies and procedures.

Over the next several months the CRP committee members went through alternating periods of elation and despair. When things were going well, they felt vindicated in the decision to take back control of the information system technology. At darker moments an angry user might ask that Troy be brought back to run a single report for an important deadline. By the end of the fiscal year, the first milestone in the new information system plan, the major challenges had been overcome. The current system was stable and under control, and there was a plan to network the entire Council and consolidate databases. The fears of traps and denunciation had proved groundless.

At this point the CRP committee began to focus more on technology and less on vision. After the executive committee approved the network plans (at slightly less cost than it would have taken for Troy and Marvin to maintain the status quo), the CRPs set about writing Requests for Proposals and interviewing vendors. The final system was a fairly sophisticated network combining all of the Macs with the Windows machines, a flexible array of printers, and shared modem and fax capabilities.

The earlier database analysis was used to create a grid that listed the different databases on one axis and the list of data elements (first name, address, etc.) along the other. The grid was then used to plan a consistent naming structure and to sort elements according to their relationship to one another. At the conclusion of the process, the many lists had become a single names file and small assortment of gift, affiliate, and membership history tables.

Ownership

In the period of five months, from the inception of the CRP committee until the funding for the network overhaul was approved, the Council went from leasing their information management system to full ownership. With minimal assistance from outside consultants, they were able to move from a position of dependency to one of control. Completing the network installation did not end the CRP committee's reason for existence. Having a centralized database does not mean that all decisions about operations have been made. A complex system requires proactive controls to insure that it adds value to agency goals. Technology has to function as a tool, not as an edifice unto itself.

Sustainability

Developing a strategy to balance the need to meet ongoing system management needs with the need to maintain the overall vision was the next challenge for the CRP committee. The executive committee, the CRP committee, and other staff liked how the system was evolving. There was no movement to institute an MIS coordinator's position yet, although the question will be revisited in the future. They agreed that it was important to promote a goal for the near future: to develop a significant knowledge base of technical and practice oriented information in order to anticipate new needs and directions in the agency. When new opportunities presented themselves, they would have a methodology in place to observe, react, and evaluate the situation. This gave the Council the freedom to institute system improvements in a flexible and controlled manner.

Case Study #3—Describing the Problem

We have found that system specifications employing terms such as "flexible," "easy to use," and "potential for growth" are usually too generic. When push comes to shove, the people writing the specs want an easy out and are not willing to operationalize their definitions. It is easy to state flexibility as a requirement; it is much harder to define it.

A regional foster care coordinating agency (the Agency) wanted to automate as much of its placement tracking as possible. Money wasn't a problem because it had been very successful in fund raising for technology and had written system development costs into several state contracts. Internally, automation was thought of as a simple and straightforward purchase of hardware, programming, evaluation, and cutover from the manual to the on-line system. The program director selected a programmer experienced in foster care and executed an open-ended contract for system consulting and development services. Four months into the project, the program director left for another position. Marsha, the office manager, whose responsibilities included supervising word processing, was put in charge of coordinating the project.

Understanding the Business Problem

The term programmer can be bit misleading. One of the best metaphors is to compare system development with building a home. In construction there is a hierarchy that starts with an architect to create the design. Next, a general contractor takes the design and plans the job, hiring carpenters and subcontractors to do the actual work. While the carpenters are the most visible part of the job, they represent a fairly minor part of the overall process. In application development there is a similar hierarchy of design, coordination, and programming. The programmers are, like carpenters, the most visible part of the process, but they require some sort of blueprint before they can begin to work. However, many programmers believe that an extensive analysis and design phase is unnecessary. They prefer to treat the project as a set of discreet problems, and the final product as the blending of multiple revisions of many different programs. But the wise home buyer would not trust a carpenter to build a whole house, deciding on the number and arrangement of rooms, traffic flow, or architectural style as the work progressed.

The programmer hired by the agency, Jack, took the approach that eliminated the architect. Marsha, who had no prior experience with database development projects, was in no position to argue at first. However, over time she began to demand increasing amounts of documentation on what the system would contain and how it would work. Jack felt that this step was unnecessary and interfered with his job, which was to write code and see if it worked. Their relationship deteriorated over time. The new program director didn't care, but tended to side with Jack as the professional. Marsha quit.

Marsha's replacement, Andrew, inherited the project. Jack took him out to lunch and explained that Andrew was supposed to stay out of his way and approve invoices as they were submitted. Andrew, overwhelmed by his new job, readily agreed. Once or twice a month Jack would come into the central office to talk to one or staff members, then disappear. Fragments of the system began to emerge. One or two staff would have a module installed, receive some training, then work with it for several weeks. Staff were generally positive, and the reports were considered exceptional.

Problems began to emerge after a while. Staff who had had special training in the testing phase could use the program, but staff in the outlying offices were having difficulties. Jack dismissed the problems as a lack of user sophistication and too much deviation from official procedures. In effect, the staff of the satellite offices were not smart enough to use the software, and even if they were, they did not follow the rules. As more data went into the program, glitches with module compatibility began to emerge. The licensing department was supposed to provide the placement department with a list of newly certified foster families, but lacked phone numbers and availability information. Similar problems emerged weekly. Jack assured everyone that the problems were minor, and that he had developed a prioritized fix-list. To staff, each fix seemed to create two new problems. The database was only 80% complete, and already it was falling apart.

The executive director did some checking. Jack, it turned out, did have foster care experiences, but only in program evaluation (which explained why the reports were so good). For general workflow issues he had relied primarily on outmoded policy and procedure documents (which explained why things didn't work in the field). It was clear that they would not be able to correct all of the system faults for the money left in budget. Jack was the only person who understood the system, so there was no question of terminating his contract. The staff responsible for hiring Jack and supervising his work through the early phase were no longer with the agency, so there was no one else to fire.

A great deal was riding on this system, so the executive director did what he felt was the only logical thing for the agency: he faked it. Individual modules worked well enough to get by, and the lack of overall coordination could be supplemented by brute force. Additional staff were hired to do the things that the program couldn't. State officials and funders would be given demonstrations of the working components, while the missing pieces would be glossed over. The agency declared victory and went on about their business.

Why Systems Fail

There was never an official post mortem for why the Agency's database failed. There seldom is—no one wants to readily admit to a series of mistakes that have cost their organization large amounts of money without providing significant value. More common is the approach taken by the Agency: ignore the problems while concentrating on what is good about the system. The traditional approach to assigning credit and blame is to say that management is responsible for the good things that happen, while staff is responsible for the failures. We tend to look at it the other way around; management is responsible for creating the opportunity, but it is the staff that makes the system work. When systems fail, it is entirely the result of management not creating the right environment for success. The following is a list of warning signs that indicate a system planning cycle is in trouble.

Personality and Responsibility

The biggest problem with any project is communication between the participants. If there are personal or administrative barriers to communication, there will not be enough information available to make decisions or evaluate results. At the Agency, the personal conflict between Marsha and Jack meant that information about the project's status was not getting to key decision-makers. Even with better information about the project, senior management's abrogation of responsibility for the supervision of system development to administrative staff meant that there would not be a central control structure. In effect, after Marsha left, no one was in charge of the system or could even influence the direction Jack was taking.

Lack of Structural Sophistication

The foster care tracking system became, in effect, Jack's personal vision of how data collection for reporting and evaluation should be done. His was a neat and orderly environment where everything had its place. He was used to dealing with data after it had been collected, so was unprepared for the way case workers had to deal with incomplete and inconsistent information every day. The system approached data collection as a linear process, while the reality of the situation was that staff had to work iteratively, sometimes going to several sources before the right information was available. Ultimately, Jack's system lacked the structural sophistication to manage the ambiguities of foster care.

Shortened Implementation Cycle

Things just happened too fast. Jack's program was embraced because it produced results early in the process. The early success did not take into account how components would fit together, so there was no perceived need to engage in strategic planning. The result of shortening the planning phase was that no comprehensive specifications were ever created. It was a situation where it would virtually cost twice as much to fix the system, because half the money would go to figuring what it already did. By not giving the programmer enough detail in the scope of work, the Agency ended up with a system that fulfilled the contract specifications, but could not easily be used in the real world.

Lack of Training

Because Jack and the staff beta testers could use the system, he assumed that anyone could. The beta testers received extensive training through their contact with Jack. Staff in the satellite offices received the software, the most perfunctory training, and little technical support.

Training is one of the key factors to the success of any system. While design, planning, programming, policies, and procedures are critical to bringing an automation or reengineering project to life, proper training and ongoing support are necessary for the system to be used as intended. Without training, enthusiasm for change in general, and the new system in particular, is rapidly lost while workers struggle to master new tools from the framework of the old way of doing things. The situation is similar to the old farmer who purchased a new-fangled chain-saw because he heard how much faster it would cut wood compared to a bow saw, but he returned it to the general store the next day as too slow. The clerk wanted to go out back to check the saw before refunding the money. The farmer agreed, and when the clerk pulled the cord to start the saw, the farmer asked, "What's that noise?"

Why Systems Work

In this chapter we have described how organizations view and manage information technology. Those at the forefront have strong leadership in either a single individual with a vision or in a team with a set of common goals. Without strong leadership you run the risk of risk of surrendering responsibility to a vendor whose goals are not necessarily consistent with those of your agency. The key factors that lead to good system development are just plain common sense and understanding of the objective: providing the right information at the right time to enhance service delivery.

One of the key factors for the Chapter's success in managing the evolution of their system from a proprietary minicomputer to a mixed and more open LAN was that the MIS director could communicate with the board at a level of detail that they could easily understand. Technical issues were never discussed, everything was couched in terms of doing work more efficiently and realizing a long-term return on investment. The Council's executive committee gave the CRPs the authority to organize their own support environment. The Agency failed because it surrendered all responsibility early in the planning process—communication ceased after the contract was signed.

Conclusion

The case studies shown illustrate several key points. Systems planning is a necessity in any setting with more than one computer and one user. You can not buy or borrow a plan; you have to build it yourself. The organization has to own the process, and not depend extensively on external resources. A wide range of staff who use the information must be involved, and they must be given enough authority to have some measurable effect. Expect that planning will be disruptive and time consuming, but understand that it can be conducted in English and remain consistent with the overall strategic plan. The pay-offs are substantial; costs for information management can be anticipated and controlled, and the quality of information (reports, proposals, statistics) meets both demands of customers—those who pay for what you do and those who benefit from your services—and internal needs for high-quality information.

19

Suggestions for Board Development

This book can be a useful reference guide for a board development program, or its use can provide at least the beginnings of a united point of view on the subject.

If you believe that your organization requires the services of a consultant, then by all means, retain a consultant. They are very useful in guiding the board through the development process while remaining a neutral party in any disagreements that may arise. But retain intelligently—there are many "consultants" who depend on rhetoric rather than talent or knowledge. It is interesting to note how much time and effort an organization will spend on searching out and hiring a consulting firm and how little time it will spend figuring out why a firm or consultant is required and what to do with them once they have been retained. This lack of precision in what is expected of counsel is perhaps the major cause of friction in the client-counsel relationship. Obviously, there are other sources, but this one stands out.

Unless an atmosphere of trust exists between the consultant and the client, it will be impossible for them to work together. Consultants step in to help, not to take over or to interfere with operations. Consultants, just like clients, want to be successful. In order to build trust, clients must be able to level with each other, to discuss the issues before the organization honestly and straightforwardly. The withholding of critical data absolutely destroys the ability of counsel to render valid assistance.

At the outset of the relationship, don't hesitate to ask questions or to make suggestions. The client-consultant relationship is not meant to be passive, responding only to the initiatives of the counsel. If asked by a consultant, don't hesitate to disclose financial information, plans, surveys, board biographies, staff information, problems, and so on. We hold all information confidential. Do not restrict access to any individual, volunteer or paid, who is a part of the organization. Many aspects of institutional knowledge rarely find their way into print, but may be of immeasurable help in the consultant's service to his client.

If client and counsel are to build trust and to make the best use of all data, each must know what is to be expected from the other. Roles must be clearly defined. Counsel's role falls into two broad categories:

1. Counsel may sit with the client and advise on what should be done. The responsibility for implementation then rests with the client.
2. Alternatively, counsel may actively participate in the implementation of plans by giving seminars, writing documents, resolving differences, solving problems, and so on.

What is required is a clear definition of who will do what—in writing.

Do not place a consultant in the position of supervising or following up on staff. This simply blurs roles and confuses issues. Consultants are best at planning, organizing, and pointing the way. Essentially, they are a catalytic agent.

Remember as well that consultants can make mistakes. Sometimes they are impractical; however, they should be listened to at all times. Challenge their conclusions and examine the concepts and processes from which they were derived. The consultant's fundamental role is to work himself or herself out of a job.

In hiring consultants, you have hired a firm and not an individual. People being people, sometimes the individual assigned by a consulting firm as your counsel simply doesn't work out because of personality differences. If you feel an individual is wrong for your organization, let the firm know in full, and in fairness. You have a right to expect supervision—the regular visitation of a senior officer of the firm for a check-up on the job. This is as helpful to the firm's personnel as it is to the client

Counsel's conclusions are not always flattering. They will not always tell you what you want to hear or point out directions you want to take. Remember the story of the emperor and his new clothes.

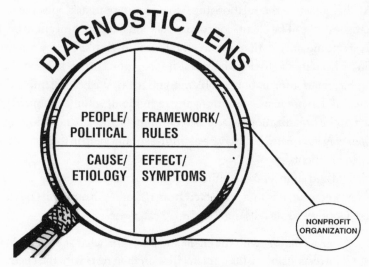

Figure 19-1. The diagnostic lens

Finally, it is important for the client to take the view that the retention of counsel is a sign of strength, not weakness. It is a wise organization that recognizes its problems and seeks assistance or retains counsel to monitor current operations from an independent perspective. No person or organization is an island.

During my years as director of programs for the Chicago Boys Clubs, I was privileged to work with Dr. Karl Menninger, who was the Director of the Boys and Girls Club of Chicago Youth Mental Health Project. The three years we worked together were the most challenging years I ever spent. He gave me an autographed copy of his book *The Vital Balance*. It contains many memorable and useful passages, such as this one, that still guide me today.

> We, the authors, *vigorously oppose* the view that *treatment, other* than first *aid,* should *proceed before or without diagnosis.* On the contrary, we feel that diagnosis is today more important than ever.
>
> Fresh from medical-school training, where they have been taught to identify diseases, they (young doctors) come into psychiatry, where they see illness and hence expect to find diseases. They want to apply labels. They seek, then, to rid the patient of this—his disease. They can scarcely wait to begin treating the patient and observing his "improvement" under their ministrations.

All too often boards leap into a process of change without thinking that process through. Dr. Karl says simply and directly, "don't jump to solutions until you have identified the issues. This is diagnosis." Here are a few suggestions on how to invigorate a board.

The issues facing our nonprofits can be diagnosed by viewing them through a *diagnostic lens.* In considering a development program for a board of directors, we must analyze the issues in the following way:

People/political We are having a problem with people (individual, intraboard, intrastaff, or board-staff).

Framework/rules The framework or rules within which we expect our board and staff to work are confusing, contradictory, or nonexistent. Be careful here. In this situation, there is a common perception that the organization simply isn't "arranged right." This statement carries the implication that one needs only to rearrange the boxes and the problem will be solved. Review chapter 1, "Point of View."

Cause Is the issue a cause of problems? Etiology means "cause."

Effect Is the issue an effect?

The importance here is knowing the difference between cause and effect. If we work only on symptoms, the effects will retain again and again. For example, the question, "How do I motivate my board?" frequently elicits the response, "By increasing our recognition procedures." This may help in the short term, but may miss the real underlying issue such as a dysfunctional recruitment and orientation system.

I like to use the dandelion metaphor. We cut off the flower and some roots and think we have gotten rid of the dandelion, but we overlook the dandelion's extensive root system. If we don't get it all, back it comes.

Problems and crises are really quite different. A crisis is simply a crucial stage at which future events are determined—a turning point. A problem is a question or situation that presents doubt, perplexity, or difficulty

Failure to solve problems inevitably leads to crisis. If the reader will allow me to shift from dandelions to world history, remember Winston Churchill during World War II. "Courage is the one quality which guarantees all others," he said. It takes courage on the part of leadership to initiate,

Figure 19-2. Dandelion metaphor—1

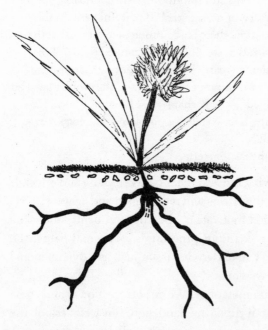

Figure 19-3. Dandelion metaphor—2

and then to support, ongoing assessment. It takes courage because the results of the assessment may not be flattering to the leadership.

But if it takes courage to initiate assessment, it takes more courage to institute change based on the results of that assessment. There is a natural tendency to rationalize results and to take no action. While this may protect individual egos, it is organizationally destructive. Remember, massive change will be met with massive resistance unless the principles of change are fully understood and employed. Effectiveness means doing the right things; efficiency means doing those things right. Writes Peter Drucker:

> Efficiency . . . means focus on costs. But the optimizing approach should focus on *effectiveness*. It focuses on opportunities to produce revenue, to create markets, and to change the economic characteristics of existing products and markets. It asks not, How do we do this or that better? It asks, which of the products really produce extraordinary economic results or are capable of producing them? Which of the markets and/or end uses are capable of producing extraordinary results? It then asks, to what results should the resources and efforts of the business be allocated so as to produce extraordinary results rather than the "ordinary" ones which is all efficiency can possibly produce?
>
> This does not deprecate efficiency. Even the healthiest business, the business with the greatest effectiveness, can well die of poor efficiency. But even the most efficient business cannot survive, let alone succeed, if it is efficient in doing the wrong things, that is, if it lacks effectiveness. No amount of efficiency would have enabled the manufacturer of buggy whips to survive.
>
> Effectiveness is the foundation of success—efficiency is a minimum condition for survival *after* success has been achieved. Efficiency is concerned with doing things right. Effectiveness is doing the right things.
>
> Efficiency concerns itself with the input of effort into *all* areas of activity. Effectiveness, however, starts out with the realization that in business, as in any other social organism, 10 or 15 percent of the phenomena— such as products, orders, customers, markets, or people—produce 80 to 90 percent of the results. The 85 to 90 percent of the phenomena, no matter how efficiently taken care of, produce nothing but costs (which are always proportionate to transactions, that is, to busy-ness).

Board development is a combined effort between board and staff. If the board decides to enter into a development program, a task force should be formed and co-chaired by the board chairperson and the executive director. A commission should be developed to tell the task force exactly what is expected of it. The commission should give specific instructions as to the advisability of retention of counsel, topics to be addressed, and time frames. Most of the time this is at least a six-month process with counsel retained for the entire time. It usually runs in three parts: preparation, a two-day workshop, and a follow-up session.

Entropy as an organizational concept is a derivative of the Second Law of Thermodynamics. Basically, it says that all organized systems will move

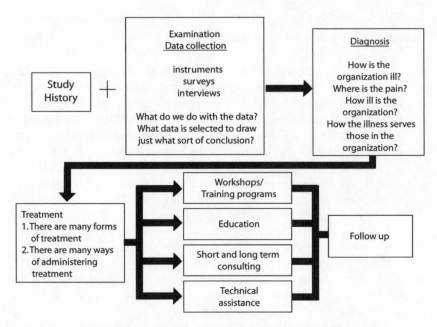

Figure 19-4. Board development process

toward chaos unless energy is brought into the system to reestablish order. In other words, everything that is organized will break down or run down unless it is maintained. Everything moves toward disorder, unless someone intentionally intervenes to reestablish order. Have you looked in your closet lately? Or perhaps at the top of your desk or your back yard? Entropy is the antithesis of growth.

In organizational life, there are many signs of entropy. Max DePree, chairman of Herman Miller, Inc., a Fortune 500 manufacturer of office systems, lists several:

1. A tendency toward superficiality
2. Tension among key people
3. No time for celebration and ritual
4. Thinking that rewards and goals are the same things
5. No longer telling the stories of the past
6. Avoidance of complexity and ambiguity
7. Problem makers outnumber problem solvers
8. Seeking to control rather than liberate
9. Pressures of today pushing aside concern for vision and risk

10. When rules, manuals and ratios replace contribution, spirit, excellence, and joy
11. When we rely on structures rather than people

Try using this list as a model to construct your own. Then apply the list to your organization to see how you rate. While you're at it, ask your board and staff what they would add. Then ask each individual to do a rating and compare results. Remember that entropy is the antithesis of growth, that renewal is the antidote for entropy, and that community (or *board*, for our purposes) is the enabler of renewal.

20

When Nonprofits
Try to Become
More Businesslike

The service institution (which includes nonprofits) will perform, it is said again and again, if only it is managed in a businesslike manner. . . . [I]f only administrators were to behave like businessmen, service institutions would perform. This belief underlies today's management boom in the service institutions. It is the wrong diagnosis and being businesslike is the wrong prescription for the ills of the service institution.

—Peter F. Drucker

In spite of this warning (among others), the belief prevails that nonprofits must become more businesslike. Furthermore, the belief prevails that nonprofit executives must be trained to be more businesslike in their management practices. The confusion engendered by these mistaken beliefs is at the heart of the current ambiguity in nonprofit management.

There is no question that nonprofits can be better managed, and we need to understand more about what better nonprofit management means.

Better nonprofit management, however, does not necessarily mean more businesslike management. Until we examine this myth (remember, all myths have a basis in fact), nonprofit volunteers and staff will continue to function with their MBAs: management by ambiguity. There are some universal management concepts, but they are not the sole property of business. What makes a business a business, however, is not the same as what makes a nonprofit a nonprofit. The real challenge before us is to make nonprofits more "nonprofitlike." But what does "nonprofitlike" really mean?

Brian O'Connell, president of the Independent Sector, illustrated this well in his remarks before the Professional Education Forum on October 31, 1984:

> Everything tracks back to our need to have clearer understanding of the unique functions of government, business and nonprofit organizations and the importance of not judging any one of the three according to standards that do not give principal emphasis to their unique role.

What has brought about all this recent activity? The reasons for the rush to make nonprofits accountable are many, and not particularly important for this book. Donors, boards of directors, and clients are all pushing nonprofits toward a greater degree of accountability. New questions are being asked of nonprofits that go to the appropriateness of funding existing programs over potential ones; to the expected results of some programs; to assessing those results; and to whether the results are cost-effective.

These new questions are a startling departure for nonprofit organizations accustomed to a satisfactory existence because they were viewed as inherently good and have long histories to prove it. Now they are being asked to earn their existence. As a result, many nonprofits are at a crossroads in their institutional lives. The choice is not simply whether to innovate and change; organizations must innovate and change because their very survival is at stake. The problem is that once those immediate survival needs are met, organizations often relax until the next crisis arises—and then the cycle repeats itself. For many nonprofits, another crisis cycle means the end of their existence. The real choice is how to institutionalize the continuous innovation and renewal needed to avoid the destructive cycles. All of this has neatly impaled today's nonprofits on a three-horned dilemma.

The Dilemma

Horn One

Because the accountability issue cannot be addressed outside the context of management, nonprofits are being asked to improve management practices. The problem is that "better management" is being equated with "reducing operating expenses." Better management is, in fact, more expensive, not less. If operating expenses are reduced, it will be only in the long-range future.

Most nonprofits are already budgetarily marginal. Insistence on better management increases costs in three significant areas:

1. *Staffing.* More, not fewer, staff are required. Nonprofit staff are already overcommitted and work long hours.
2. *Technology.* Technology is not cheap. Although initial costs for computer purchases are nominal these days, maintenance, programming, operators, and software are expensive.
3. *Education, training, consulting.* When budget reductions are made, it is staff development expenses that go first.

Horn Two

There is a threat—the rise of interest in "earned income." While earned income programs are not without merit, there is a danger that many nonprofits will view profit-based activities as a financial panacea. If this tendency is carried too far, the earned income fad may undermine the basic premise of voluntarism—citizen participation. At least one consultant has suggested that this trend requires a new form of organization, a "fourth sector," as it were, that would be a blend of the for-profit and nonprofit organization. We do not need another organizational concept to further confuse the issue, that is, how to make the current nonprofit model work by adapting it to a changing environment. There is nothing wrong with the nonprofit concept—only what we have done with it.

Horn one, increased and expensive expectations of accountability, coupled with horn two, dwindling resources, form a deadly dilemma. Add horn three, and the problem reaches destructive proportions.

Horn Three

Twenty years ago, interest in nonprofit management was negligible. Since then, interest has increased geometrically. The field of nonprofit management has been flooded with books, pamphlets, journals, and a variety of other written, audio, and video material. The number of colleges and universities offering some type of nonprofit management curriculum, whether degree-based or certificate-based, has grown from a mere handful a few years ago to more than four hundred today. Few of these institutions, however, are quite sure of what to teach.

Consultants have crowded the nonprofit scene. It has become the *new* cottage industry. Consulting ranges from management assistance programs within the United Way, through local and national nonprofit management support organizations, to hundreds of individual consultants. In any given week, a nonprofit executive can expect to receive a dozen brochures for workshops or seminars proclaiming solutions to this or that management ill.

There is quantity—the problem is quality. There are important and useful materials and workshops, but they are individual works; they are not integrated into a conceptual model of the nonprofit organization. The most dismaying aspect of this flood of advice is its generally superficial approach to solving nonprofit management problems. Assistance tends to be directed at symptoms, not causes. Consultants, publications, and the curricula of higher education rush to treatment, almost completely bypassing diagnosis. There are many forms of treatment and many ways of administering it, but even more important than treatment is skillful diagnosis.

The fundamental problem, however, is the lack of a *comprehensive* or integrated model of nonprofit management that demonstrates the uniqueness of the nonprofit organization. Many aspects of nonprofit management have been studied and written about. There has been, however, no holistic approach. For a nonprofit to become "accountable" in the management sense, there must first be a holistic management model to describe what it is that must be managed and held accountable.

Adaptation or Adoption?

We have, in effect, a nonprofit management vacuum. We know that nature abhors a vacuum and will do anything to fill it. Business administration and, to a lesser degree, public administration have rushed in to fill the void.

From this scene of chaos comes the exhortation that nonprofits must become more businesslike. The message? *Adopt* businesslike practices. But why not *adapt*? Unfortunately, because no one is quite sure what makes a nonprofit a nonprofit, what should be selective adaptation becomes wholesale adoption.

All of this leaves the nonprofit executive—and board member—in confusion. The mixed messages, conflicting material, and narrowly focused opinions render it difficult for the nonprofit executive and board member to make informed management choices.

Of equal importance is the difficulty this state of affairs creates for donors trying to make informed choices about charitable contributions. The ambiguity of standards makes it difficult to evaluate an organization against itself and against accepted nonprofit management criteria (i.e., nonprofitlike).

Finally, nonprofits themselves create some of the confusion. Community organizations, for example, will argue that they cannot be evaluated by the same standards used for human service organizations. This is not pluralism. It is separatism. What nonprofits require is a common conceptual model that encompasses a multitude of organizational purposes and forms.

Business falls sadly short as a role model. For all that has been written about business administration and for all the thousands of MBAs that business schools have churned out, the business landscape is still cluttered with failures. We hear constant laments over the loss of competitive position and reduced productivity. The fact is that very few businesses show consistent growth over the long haul.

By using business as a role model, we force on nonprofits business practices that may be useful to business, but may be fatal to nonprofits. For example, too many board members and staff come into conflict because they have not taken into consideration the fact that the culture of the nonprofit is generally different from the culture of the corporation. This does not mean that one or the other is wrong, only that they are different.

Many nonprofits are adopting (through board insistence) business staff titles: president, vice president, and so on. The worst abuse of this practice is the use of the term chief executive officer (CEO). In the corporate sense of the word, the CEO often is both the head of the board of directors and the head of the employees. When the title of CEO is applied to the executive of a nonprofit, there is an inherent supposition that the nonprofit executive is responsible for the performance of the board. This, of course, is not true.

In point of fact, the nonprofit has two CEOs—one for the board and one for the staff. They work together closely, but one does not give direct leadership to the other's group nor should one be held accountable for the performance of the other's group. The relationship is a perfect example of symbiosis.

Some time ago, I attended a conference on professional education in colleges and universities. There were some thirty universities or colleges represented, as well as practitioners and foundation representatives. One panel consisted of a practitioner and two individuals from prominent universities who were involved in nonprofit education. One panelist made the astounding observation that the boards of directors of nonprofit and for-profit organizations do the same thing. My astonishment was compounded when the other two panelists agreed, and not one person in the audience of about one hundred protested. In fact, I saw a lot of heads nod in agreement.

I have studied, served on, and written about nonprofit boards for years. We continually trumpet the uniqueness of the voluntary spirit and the nonprofit organization. If this is true, how can we maintain the fiction that business and nonprofit boards do the same things? I can support the general statement that business boards and nonprofit boards share one general function—that is, they both set policy. There are dramatic differences, however, in the definition of policy, the board policy process, the relationship of the executive director and chairperson of the board, the relationship of the board and staff, the nature of measurement and evaluation, the sharing of the implementation of board policy by the board and staff, the job description or role of the board member, and the culture created by the voluntary spirit. Unless these are clearly defined, there is no hope of orderly governance.

Finally, we come to financials. Nonprofit financial statements cannot be interpreted by the same rules as business financials. Business people must learn a whole new set of concepts, vocabulary, and financial standards. They must learn that standard business operating ratios do not apply. For example, if the business financial statement shows a profit, it can be assumed that the business is not only being efficiently run, but is doing what it ought to do. It is effective, as sales are directly tied to product.

A nonprofit financial statement, too, can be balanced, also demonstrating efficiency. But at the same time that it is efficient, it can be totally ineffective. The key is fund-raising. Until recently, raising money had only a marginal relationship to effectiveness. I have come across many organizations that were great fund-raisers; the problem was that I had a difficult time figuring out just what they were doing.

In sum, we must create our own nonprofit identity. We must have a nonprofit management concept within which we identify our own tasks and responsibilities. We must avoid fads and build a solid conceptual foundation upon which to base our practice. We must use the best of our two sister sectors, business and public. Let us adopt what we can, adapt what we must. The donor community must increase its inspection of current nonprofit consulting practices and increase its support of nonprofit management consulting. This can begin by discarding the misleading term "technical assistance."

We must make a clear distinction between management and leadership. A nonprofit cannot survive without both. It is management that keeps the nonprofit train on the tracks. It is leadership, however, that lays those tracks. The most patronizing things in all voluntarism are those book titles and workshop descriptions that include "managing volunteers." We must never forget:

- We manage things.
- We lead people.

21

Conclusions

In this book, I hope we have blended art and science, remembering that art without science becomes manipulation and science without art becomes autocracy. I have written this book based on the premise that people, if asked to do meaningful work for a believable cause in an understanding framework, will respond. Harold J. Seymour said it best:

> But all in all, I would beg you to believe—as I do now and always have—that most people are very wonderful indeed, that they almost always wish to do the right thing, and that their ultimate performance, when boldly challenged and confidently led, is usually far better than we have any right to expect. Study them and treat them well, for you need them more than money.

I do not claim that everything I have written has worked for everybody; but everything I have written has worked in many places. I do not claim that the ideas are necessarily new; the past has been a good teacher. This book is a blend of new and old ideas presented in new ways and with new applications, based on 24 years of practice and helping hundreds of individuals to wing it.

I wish to leave you with a word about democracy. A democratic society will exist only to the degree that voluntarism is viable. Each of the following statements about democracy has voluntarism at its core:

> "Democracy is both the best and the most difficult form of political organization—the most difficult because it is the best." (Ralph Benton Perry)

> "Men have always found it easy to be governed. What is hard is for them to govern themselves."

> "Of the many things we have done to democracy in the past, the worst has been the indignity of taking it for granted." (Max Lerner)

> "Today we all realize that democracy is not a self-perpetuating virus adapted to any body politic—that was the assumption of a previous generation. Democracy we now know to be a special type of organism requiring specific nutriment materials—some economic, some social and cultural." (James B. Conant)

Democracy! No other political system offers such opportunity for individual and social fulfillment simultaneously. No other system provides for those who govern to be supervised by and held accountable to those who are governed.

Yet this system, which provides both for individual freedom and for the collective good, contains within itself the seeds of its own destruction. As more and more individuals attain success—in whatever form they perceive success—subtle changes begin to erode the promise of a democratic society. These changes give birth to two situations that characterize sclerotic, moribund democracy: unenlightened self-interest and selective democracy.

Unenlightened self-interest is characterized by the rise of materialism at the expense of intellectual and spiritual values. Self-gratification at any cost dominates. "What's in it for me?" (at the expense of others) becomes a common attitude. There is a tendency to enjoy what has been achieved. Motivation to action is primarily for "more" and "better," regardless of side effects. Special-interest groups grow stronger as individuals band together for greater leverage. Adversarial relationships replace collaboration. Yet the vast majority doze off in front of the television set or survey society from the ostrich position.

Selective democracy is the result of a desire on the part of the majority to consolidate and protect their gains. Prosperity comes at the expense of others. Democracy becomes the means to deprive other individuals or groups of their economic, educational, and political rights. The very system that guarantees these rights philosophically is used to withhold those same rights operationally. While this book is not, of course, a study of democracy, the warnings of Perry, Lerner, and Conant—as well as the following caution from Saul Alinsky—have all played a role:

> There can be no democracy unless it is a dynamic democracy. When our people cease to participate—to have a place in the sun—then all of us will wither in the darkness of decadence. All of us will become mute, demoralized lost souls.

These words are all saying something very significant. We must work within the system, not *replace* it. Although the ever-rising cry is to abolish the system, the problems and evils of democracy are not inherent; its deficiencies are found not in the concept itself, but in its practice. To make the system work, we must begin with *people,* and people's attitudes are largely determined by the societal conditions in which they find themselves. Gardner puts it this way:

> As a society (or institution) matures there is a subtle but pervasive shift in attitudes toward what is possible. The youthful attitude that "anything is possible" is encountered less frequently, and there are more experts on why "it can't be done." The consequences are predictable: fewer mistakes—and less innovation. Confidence born of ignorance and inexperience is not so contemptible a quality as some imagine.
>
> But of course life cannot be lived in utter disregard of the real limitations that surround performance. And in fact the appraisals which most people make of the limits of the possible are based on some solid evidence. The fatalism of the Asian peasant is not really surprising, in view of the evidence before him. Men will harbor a hopeful view of what man can achieve only if their societies do, in fact, offer some scope for individual accomplishment. If their societies provide them with the opportunity to grow as individuals and to have an impact on their environment, their attitudes will reflect those realities.

At the heart of this is our voluntary boards. The cry is heard ever more loudly that the board concept is an anachronism and should be drastically altered or abolished. This would be a tragic approach; for boards, with their concept of citizen involvement, are fundamental to democracy. True,

they are complex and difficult to operate effectively. The rewards, however, are worth the effort.

For a board to be effective, special effort and understanding are required on the part of staff and board volunteers. If both are willing to work
at the concept within the parameters outlined in this book, we will have successful boards, successful organizations, and a strengthened democracy.
Our voluntary organizations will prosper.

Today's economic environment tends to dictate "cutbacks" while donors, board members, and clients are demanding better quality or services,
higher accountability, and better leadership and management. All these
things are expensive. The nonprofit professional is, justifiably, confused.
So, how do we make these choices?

We can either respond to the dilemma in a positive fashion, viewing the
situation as an opportunity for transition, or negatively, letting frustration,
stress, and depression sink morale and productivity. Negative responses include the urge to subject every department or activity to the same across-
the-board budget cut; the knee-jerk elimination of everything that does not
have an identity, is new or experimental, or earns little income; or reducing
payroll, firing those last hired even though they might be the ones best-
equipped to help manage difficult periods. Adversarial relations can easily
develop in these situations. It is particularly unproductive when threats,
picketing, or mobilization of clients and staff are used to combat downsizing. There is also an increasingly strident call for nonprofits to become more
businesslike that must be resisted—nonprofits are not businesses. Seeking
technical assistance can seem like a positive response (it sometimes is), but
most of the time you find out what you already knew, having wasted time
and money without coming any closer to a solution.

Instead, it is time to reassess programs. Prioritize essential programs
(those which are absolutely indispensable to the organization's purpose).
Assess how selected programs are being implemented. Ask yourself *"If we
were not doing it, would we do it now?"* If the answer is no, it does not matter
how well you are implementing a program—you do not need it. Finally, re-
assessment may include the purpose of the organization. The purpose may
not have been looked at for many years and may need updating.

Also consider better program models. Are there better models or more
cost-efficient means of program delivery? Restructuring and reorganizing can
be stressful, painful, and demoralizing; however, it is an essential consideration.

Try to expand and diversify your resources. Revenue is generated by nonprofits in three areas: contributions (annual, planned, and capital giving), government grants and contracts, and earned income. Nonprofits must reach a balance in all three areas. Over-dependence on one will lessen the chances of nonprofit success.

Advocacy efforts must be increased to protect nonprofit tax benefits, expanding them if possible. Efforts must also be directed at retaining as many government programs as possible. In this area, organizations such as the Independent Sector provide excellent leadership.

Increase volunteer participation and effectiveness. It is ironic that the tide of government money from the middle sixties through the seventies actually eroded volunteer participation. This had two effects. First, securing government funds became primarily a staff activity. Boards of directors tended to let staff get the grants. This lessened the willingness of boards to assume income generation responsibility. Second, with increased funding there was a tendency to hire staff rather than to involve volunteers. When substantial budget cutbacks occur, staff members sometimes return to volunteer status. This includes program, administrative, advisory, and board volunteers. Volunteers themselves must take responsibility for their own effectiveness.

Of particular importance is the training of the board chairperson or president. He or she is the leader of the board and is accountable for its effectiveness. Increased volunteer participation is the key to upsizing and upgrading in an environment which suggests the opposite.

Also look to cooperative programs to reduce expenses. Nonprofits must achieve economies of scale among themselves without jeopardizing independence of thought and action. It must be noted, however, that in some cases mergers will be clearly indicated and should take place.

Do some strategic planning. Take the long view. As difficult as it is, view the downsizing process in the context of a future you have designed for yourself. You are not only managing for today, but you are setting the foundation for your future. Do not forget your vision.

Avoid the activity trap. Years ago, when I was the youth work secretary (an old YMCA professional designation) of the Addison Road Branch of the Cleveland YMCA, I had an executive vice president of the Stouffer's Company as my program committee chairperson. We were in a planning meeting for the following year's objectives. I was projecting membership numbers and attendance at our various activities.

My chairperson said that these were interesting and useful, but were only part of the question. He asked why I had selected those particular activities and what behavioral change or improvement I expected from a young person's participation in the activities. The lesson, of course, was not to confuse means with ends.

The nonprofit sector exists solely to deal with the deficiencies of its sister sectors, business and government. The only way to justify the existence of a nonprofit is to the extent it does in fact deal with deficiencies through objectives and outcomes

If things are truly desperate, universal salary reductions are better than the elimination of jobs. This will reduce the budget and may preserve needed jobs. It could also result in a more unified staff, as all will be sacrificing a bit rather than a few sacrificing everything. Job responsibilities of released staff are often merely transferred to those who remain, decreasing an organization's efficiency.

Technical assistance doesn't always help, especially without asking a number of questions first. Asking board and staff to have clear answers as to why technical assistance seems necessary, whether they can list specific issues that the technical assistance is to address, and what results it is to provide is a good start. Only then should the provider be considered, taking into account how the provider's credentials are to be assessed. Once the technicians arrive, their work must be monitored—what sort of benchmarks can a nonprofit use?

Consider the seven deadly tendencies in nonprofit technical assistance:

1. The tendency to say, "Just tell me how to do it." We are in the age of formulas. The principles and concepts which underlie how-to are ignored in the search for a formula. This renders the nonprofit professional and volunteer dependent, because they must find additional resources when the old formula no longer works. Only thinking based on concepts and principles sets the human service professional free. Each professional must have an understanding that works for himself or herself. Perhaps the only constant is that each situation has its own variables and must be considered individually.

2. The tendency to be activity oriented. Attendance at training programs or the retaining of consultants is often the end. Expectations or results are often ignored. Even if results are expected, they are often not measured. The activity alone suffices.

3. The tendency to go with what is cheapest. If you have $5,000 to spend, isn't it better to go with a consultant who will give twenty days for that amount rather than one who will give ten days? Cost is not always an indicator of quality.

4. The tendency to accept experts and publications uncritically. Because many professionals and volunteers have little in the way of a frame of reference to evaluate what is heard or read, they are often too accepting. Confusion sets in when experts offer conflicting opinions.

5. The tendency to treat symptoms rather than causes. We must learn to diagnose. Many consultants and workshops treat only symptoms, not underlying causes. A cadre of consultants, workshop leaders, and authors who are experts in one or two areas of human service leadership can still lack an overall view. Publications often treat problems according to their own specialty, without proper diagnosis. Many times problems within a specialty are a symptom of a much larger systemic problem. Even when the symptom is temporarily relieved, the problem always reemerges.

6. The tendency to correct weaknesses rather than build on strengths. Many planning programs begin with what is called a management audit. This is a device to identify strengths and weaknesses (sometimes weaknesses are called "blocks"). The idea is to correct the weaknesses and move on. This inordinate attention to weakness often becomes a self-fulfilling prophecy. What may look like weakness may, in fact, be a source of great strength. Weakness often is the result of an overextension of strength. It is far better to identify our strengths, feel good about ourselves, and then begin to plan. If the planning process is effective, weaknesses will automatically be corrected in their proper context. A variation on this is the *SWOT* process. SWOT stands for:

   Strengths
   Weaknesses
   Opportunities
   Threats

   This process suffers from the same problem: an overemphasis on weaknesses and threats.

7. Finally, the tendency to attend technical assistance programs in hopes of learning everything necessary to solve a problem. This simply does not happen. No program can "fix" people—people "fix" themselves.

The key to answering all these issues is the preparation of our nonprofit professionals, board members, and donors. This is the issue which transcends all others and provides the framework for our solution. New professionals must be educated, just as reeducation for current professionals and the continuing development of all professionals must be seen to.

I know of no human enterprise that is more difficult to organize and lead than the nonprofit board of directors. It requires the skills of a professional and the patience of a saint. Yet a board that functions well is the most valuable resource a nonprofit organization has, and it must be nurtured well.

Appendix

Years ago, I came across a paper by William Ryan who, at that time, headed Child and Family Services of the State of Illinois. It is an impressive document, worthy, in my opinion, of being part of this book. Readers of Mr. Ryan's letter must remember that it was written in 1968 and that some of the references are outdated. The underlying principles he espouses are timeless.

The philosophical premises of citizen involvement is a re-examination of the helping process as carried out by all helping professions at all levels from local to national. Three unexpected conclusions emerge from this re-examination and may be viewed as premises for my argument.

They are:

- Social service agencies in this state [Illinois] and the nation have been able to trust only the visible tip of the iceberg, the bare surface of the total suffering and need of children, families, and communities.
- There will never be enough professionals, nor sufficient tax revenue, to adequately treat deprived families.
- It remains with the community—citizens themselves—to share responsibility. The community share is larger than we can imagine. Only citizens themselves, through their own councils and mobilized communities, by attacking social problems, developing resources, creating

prevention programs, and giving direct one-to-one and advocate help, can meet the overall responsibility, even with the help of service professionals.

We must first admit certain failure. Social agencies, psychiatry and psychological associations, naturally emphasize the numbers of people helped. Slick brochures and fancy annual reports, traditional requirements for effective public relations and continued funding, have emphasized this. The statistics the present are often accurate and these agencies truly have reason to be proud of their accomplishments. Most everything they do is achieved with limited manpower, and they deserve credit for the quality of their professional services. Of course, it is impossible to put equal emphasis on the *tens* of thousands they were *unable* to help. It is a statistical truth that only one in four of the poor receive public assistance, or welfare. The rest? They live a hand to mouth existence, begging or simply staying malnourished, ill-housed, cold—poor. Only one in six children is identified as needing day care. The larger part of this need, the part of the iceberg below the water line, receives inadequate custodial care and no educational development from neighbors or relatives. Worse, they are often left at home while parents work. A National Institute of Mental Health study showed that only one percent of emotionally disturbed children needing professional treatment received it. The community mental health approach has certainly raised this figure—*but about the top of the iceberg, there can still be no doubt.*

Ever-increasing family turmoil and breakdown lead to more child abuse, neglect of disturbed children, more foster-home placements—but what professional programs are geared to help the family *before* these crises arise? There are a few small projects here, but aside from these, practically none. It is the same in nearly all areas of need wherein the service consists of providing care, time, and, most importantly, a helping (therapeutic) human relationship. The first premise, which in no way minimizes the effective work done by thousands of dedicated professionals, nevertheless views the *totality* of need in light of our deficient collective capacity. It is time to publicly admit the harsh reality. We are failing. Professionals alone can only address a minimum human need, only the tip of the iceberg.

Admitting the problem is the first step to finding its solution. Securing tax funds means going to legislatures and private funding bodies with the necessary hyperbole: "Just give us five (or 50 or 100) more professionals and we will meet all the problems." This should never be understood to demean the need for professionals, but we could double or tripe or quintuple the number of professionals, or even the amount of public funding, and it would still not be enough to meet the gamut of needs. In other words, while government and professionals feel (and nobly push for progress based on this sentiment) that the primary responsibility for helping people, the reality is that the entire is irrational. The answer to the American dream of providing adequate material benefits—food, clothing, housing—and adequate family and individual counseling, psychiatric care and other assistance based on human relationships, will *never* be realized by sole reliance on professionals and government. The approach adopted for the past twenty-five years is a garden path to disillusionment.

The only rational alternative is citizen involvement. It is the citizen and the local community who must assume the primary responsibility for people in need. But citizens have not felt this responsibility. On viewing a child in need, for example, the average citizen has been prey to faulty thinking: "If I do help that child in need, then I am a noble, charitable soul. If I don't help that person, well, I pay my taxes anyway so that the government and professionals can help him. So, either way, I can help or not help, and I am still a good guy. All is well with the world." The average citizen has not *felt* the kind of responsibility for helping that is binding and necessary to his human fulfillment. Rather, he has been culturally attuned to feel a slight nudge to be "charitable" from time to time. But charity as typically understood has not been seen as a necessity, a binding reality. Charity can be taken or left, done or not done. The conclusion, the necessity for citizen and community *responsibility*, is based on statistical fact. It necessitates total rearrangement of much of our traditional thinking and programming to help people in need.

If there is a way to help all people in need, the basic approach must be one of bringing together citizen resources, material, and personnel to answer massive need. Methodologically, helping people must couple massive community organization to the individual case approach predominantly used today.

Maximum, effective, and genuine involvement of all citizens is the objective. Drawing analogy with the *1964 OEO concept* of "maximum feasible participation of the poor" may be helpful. Participation is not enough—involvement is essential. Involvement means action. The involvement must be genuine, that is, involvement beyond mere participation and taking the form of production—involvement that is giving of the self in place of simple bodies in attendance. The adjective "effective" must replace the word "feasible" to demonstrate the need for action with demonstrable effects. If citizens are to secure satisfaction, the basic payment is their effects: the result of their own work, the sacrifice of time, energy, thought, and money. Involvement of *all citizens* also needs emphasis. The "poor power" concept of OEO, like "money power" or "affluent power," is equally exclusive and elitist and has only been marginally successful. We must continue to organize the poor and encourage giving by the affluent, but our conclusion in relation to the *American ideal of helping all in need* is that any citizen involvement community organization effort that aims at less than genuine action collectively undertaken by all citizens will prove divisive and of limited effectiveness.

The task, therefore, is to realign the roles of citizen and professional. The helping *process*—the awareness of human dynamics and behavior, mental mechanisms, group forces, etc.—is clearly the major role of the professional. This is his basic offering; this is what he has been educated and paid for. The love component—whether known as "caring," "a helping relationship," "unconditional positive regard," or *cathexis* is that part of the process transcending knowledge, drawn from the inner recesses of the human spirit. This is the role of the citizens. The task, therefore, is to realign roles to maximize the delivery of knowledge by professionals to citizens in order to help them deliver love, caring, involvement, and action in the service of others. Love as the universal, basic drive and highest goal of all human action, must be openly and deliberately sought, built into every action of every citizen group. Apart from material need, love is the essence of the helping relationship. This is what citizens have to offer, professionals do not have a corner on the market on this capacity.

The realignment of roles and the reinstatement of citizen responsibility in the helping process mean, we must literally reverse the seat of felt responsibility, shifting it away from government and professionals back to citizens and communities where it before the rapid growth of the helping professions, back those who have any possibility for success.

Seeking massive citizen involvement cannot be continued in the same naïve way by crying, "Get involved! Get involved!" It must be recognized that we face a problem of national scope and overwhelming complexity. This problem goes by many names: depersonalization, alienation, dehumanization, malaise, and apathy all mitigate against every effort to win the massive levels of citizen involvement necessary. People are tuned out and turned off to such a degree that they often admit, "I simply don't want to get involved." Aiming for massive involvement requires reversing this depersonalization and alienation. The goal seems grandiose, even impossible. Yet, logic dictates no other course. The problems of a child in need cannot be resolved without reversing the depersonalization of the hurting society in which he lives. The question cannot be "Can we do it?" The question must be, "Is there any alternative to taking deliberate steps to resolve this gigantic problem?" Our goal is not grandiose if massive involvement is the sole alternative.

The predominant approach has been individual treatment. Against massive need, the bulk of the iceberg, it is obvious that this predominant approach will not work. The majority of collective manpower, with citizen and professional manpower merged, must be shifted away from crisis management to prevention, away from the individual case, to multiplied effort in primary prevention and citizen group approaches to broader social problems surrounding individual cases.

Serious effort to enter the area of primary prevention begins with the admission that prevention largely a cliché. In fact, we know very little about how to *prevent* something. Restructuring roles so that citizens assume their responsibility, act and obtain results, will require the government to provide the structures, channels of communication, and technical assistance so citizens can act, whether by citizens' committees, task forces, or councils. Only through mobilized citizenry can genuine and effective prevention of any significant scope be undertaken. Given massive citizen manpower and involvement, professionals will be free to undertake serious study of prevention to discover its workings.

If the seat of responsibility rests with citizens—and if maximum, effective, and genuine involvement of all citizens is to be accomplished—then the role and responsibilities of human service agency professionals must be revamped accordingly. It is not enough for government and professionals to acknowledge present system failures by saying, "Okay, we admit we can't do it, so we'll quit and simply dump the responsibility back on citizens." Rather, the strengths of both government agencies and citizens must be balanced. Government agencies and professionals must provide the channels of communication, organizational structures, and the professional and technical assistance necessary to enable citizens to effectively carry out their responsibility.

Logically necessity dictates that each and every agency should form citizens' committees, councils, task forces or boards into a network through which citizens can organize their efforts and resources. These organizations, if established under the auspices of government, would allow the citizens not only to be involved in government, but actually an *integrated part* of government.

Professionals must consistently explain the social problems that surround, and even cause individual and family problems—and the statistics and helpful methods bearing upon those problems must be consistently fed in and explained to citizens by professionals. This would logically necessitate each agency providing large amounts of staff assistance in the form of professional community organizers, and other staff to provide technical assistance and information that will enable citizens to identify and understand social problems and human behavior sufficiently to do something about them.

The logic of citizen responsibility also dictates the principles according to which each agency would have to follow in establishing the citizens' committees or councils. If citizens are to be asked to assume primary responsibility, to use their personal resources, then it follows that they have the right to determine how that responsibility is to be carried out. Self-determination includes the right to identify their own needs and setting their own priorities for action. Whereas the agency, through its staff organizer or technical assistant is responsible for providing professional knowledge to *enable* citizens to decide, it is citizens' decision. Maximum citizen involvement dictates that the organizational base of established citizens' committees, councils, and task forces be democratically constituted, comprised of the broadest possible representation of *all* citizens of the community, and that no specialized segment (whether rich, poor, black, white, rural, urban, young, old, male, female) have more than its fair share of decision-making power.

There is so little genuine involvement at this point in the history of human services that debates about elective vs. appointment vs. quota systems of selecting representation seem to be empty intellectualizations. Several guiding principles are useful in any case. In a government-sponsored citizens' committee, citizens and communities must share in the process of committee formation; executive accountability for citizens' committees that are a part of the agency, and citizens' right to the representation they choose, must be both recognized and balanced; citizens assuming responsibility will be hampered, if not forgotten, if either professionals or government officials have votes in a citizens' committee, as both groups would inevitably fall back into the old pattern of "let the professionals or the officials do it"; rather, the committees must be composed entirely of citizens, with professionals and government officials providing the specialized knowledge on an advisory basis. Instead of citizens advising government, government officials and professionals serve as advisors to citizens. This new balance returns the government and citizen relationship to the ideal long preached but rarely practiced: that government should do for the people only what the people cannot do themselves.

This way of redefining roles in human services, viewed as a whole over time, quite obviously, new ideas of the helping process, and changes in the roles of social workers, psychologists, psychiatrists, and other professional care providers. The meaning and direction of this "revolution" can be conveyed only by reviving phrases that have fallen into disrepute today, phrases like "love one another," and "neighbors helping neighbors."

Complex-sounding sociological phenomenon, like "depersonalization" and "alienation," when superfluous abstractions are called away, shows how neighbors, care about, help, and love one another—or how they become afraid to. The cure for alienation and depersonalization—national collective withdrawal from one another, is collective love, collective dependence on neighbors with neighbors. Those who are able—agencies, government, professionals—have the responsibility to provide the organizational structures and technical assistance to citizens. Enough organization, with new focus on citizen responsibility and a direct approach to neighbor helping neighbor, love, can replace depersonalization with personalization and alienation with loving involvement.

Social problems are not solved by lengthy statistics and impressive charts, but by involved people who believe that they are indeed their brother's keeper. So, too, people's individual problems are not solved by "blaming the victim" of social problems, the individual client, by subjecting them, to psychotherapy and casework with no attempt to solve the social problems. When thousands of individual casework clients—the delinquent, the neurotic adult, the disturbed teenager, the broken family or the aged isolate—voice such feelings as "I am worthless," or "Nobody cares," or "I hate everybody and everybody hates me," or "If you care or try, you get hurt," they are not only unburdening themselves, they are pinpointing the very problems they are victims of. Clients cannot be helped without also helping the uncaring society that causes his problems. Solution to human problems, whether individual or societal, requires systematic citizen organization. But genuine citizen organization, now a rare phenomenon, must become the predominant means to help people in need.

William Ryan
Child and Family Services
State of Illinois

Selected Bibliography and Suggestions for Further Reading

Books and Journal Articles

Abbott, Charles C. *Governance—A Guide for Trustees and Directors.* Boston: The Cheswick Center, 1979.

Alexander, John O. "Planning and Management in Nonprofit Organizations." In *The Nonprofit Organization Handbook,* edited by Tracy D. Connors. New York: McGraw-Hill, 1980.

Andringa, Robert C., and Ted W. Engstrom. *Nonprofit Answer Book.* Washington, D.C.: National Center For Nonprofit Boards.

Arkansas Department of Human Services. *Management Guide for Arkansas Nonprofit Organizations.* Arkansas Department of Human Services, 1987.

Axelrod, Nancy. *The Chief Executive's Role in Developing the Nonprofit Board.* Washington, D.C.: National Center for Nonprofit Boards, 1988.

———. *A Guide for New Trustees.* Washington, D.C.: Association of Governing Boards of Universities and Colleges, 1982.

Barber, Putnam, Dorothy P. Craig, Jo Larsen, and Nancy S. Notedhoff. *Fundamental Practices for Success with Volunteer Boards.* Seattle: Funprax Associates, 1982.

Behn, Robert D., and James W. Vaupel. *Quick Analysis for Busy Decision Makers.* New York: Basic Books, 1982.

Carver, John. *Boards That Make a Difference.* San Francisco: Jossey-Bass Publishers, 1981.

Chait, Richard P., and Barbara E. Taylor. "Charting the Territory of Nonprofit Boards." *Harvard Business Review* (January–February 1989).

Church, David M. *How to Succeed with Volunteers.* New York: National Public Relations Council of Health & Welfare Services, 1962.

Cleary, Robert E. "Something Personal About It." *AGB Reports* 22, no. 2 (March–April 1980): 39–42.

Connors, Tracy D. *The Nonprofit Management Handbook.* New York: John Wiley & Sons, 1993.

Council of Better Business Bureaus. *The Responsibilities of a Nonprofit Organization's Volunteer Board.* Arlington, Va.: Council of Better Business Bureaus, 1988.

———. *Standards for Charitable Solicitation.* Arlington, Va.: Council of Better Business Bureaus, 1982.

Curti, Merle. "American Philanthropy and the National Character." *American Quarterly* 10 (winter 1958): 420–37.

Dayton, Kenneth W. *Governance Is Governance.* Washington, D.C.: Independent Sector, 1987.

Didactic Systems, Inc. *The Citizen Board in Voluntary Agencies.* United Way of America, 1979.

Drucker, Peter F. *Managing the Nonprofit Organization.* New York: HarperCollins Publishers, 1990.

———. "Managing the 'Third Sector.'" *Wall Street Journal,* October 3, 1978.

———. "What Business Can Learn from Nonprofits." *Harvard Business Review* (July–August 1989).

Eberhardt, Louise. "Holding Productive and Satisfying Board Meetings." In *The Nonprofit Board Book.* Independent Community Consultants, 1985.

Flanagan, Joan. *The Successful Volunteer Organization.* Chicago: Contemporary Books, 1981.

Fram, Eugene H. "Nonprofit Boards: They're Going Corporate." In *Board Leadership and Governance.* The Society for Nonprofit Organizations, 1989.

Francis, Dave, and Mike Woodcock. *People at Work.* University Associates, 1975.

Gale, Robert L. *Building a More Effective Board.* Washington, D.C.: Association of Governing Boards of Universities and Colleges, 1984.

Gardner, John W. "The Independent Sector." In *America's Voluntary Spirit,* compiled by Brian O'Connell. New York: The Foundation Center, 1983.

Gardner, John W. *Self-Renewal: The Individual and the Innovative Society.* New York: Harper and Row, 1964.

Gidron, Benjamin, Ralph M. Kramer, and Lester M. Salamon. *Government and The Third Sector: Emerging Relationships in Welfare States.* San Francisco: Jossey-Bass Publishers, 1992.

Greenleaf, Robert K. *Servant Leadership: A Journey into the Nature of Legitimate Power and Greatness.* Mahway, N.J.: Paulist Press, 1991.

Hanson, Pauline L., and Carolyn T. Marmaduke. *The Board Member– Decision-Maker for the Nonprofit Corporation.* Sacramento, Calif.: Han-Mar Publications, 1972.

Hardy, James M. *Developing Dynamic Boards.* Erwin, Tenn.: Essex Press, 1990.

———. *Corporate Board Orientation: A Ministry of Service.* Volunteers of America, 1986.

———. *Managing for Impact in Nonprofit Organizations: Corporate Planning Techniques and Applications.* Erwin, Tenn.: Essex Press, 1984.

Herman, Robert D. *The Jossey-Bass Handbook of Nonprofit Leadership and Management.* San Francisco: Jossey-Bass Publishers, 1994.

Hodgett, R. M., and M. S. Wortman, Jr. "Decisions at Different Policy Levels." In "Charting the Territory of Nonprofit Boards," by Richard P. Chait and Barbara E. Taylor. *Harvard Business Review* (January–February 1989).

Houle, Cyril O. *Governing Boards.* San Francisco: Jossey-Bass Publishers, 1989.

———. *The Effective Board.* New York: Association Press, 1960.

Howe, Fisher. *Fund Raising and the Nonprofit Board Member.* Washington, D.C.: National Center for Nonprofit Boards, 1988.

Jacobsen, Ann, ed. *Standards and Guidelines for the Field of Voluntarism.* Association of Volunteer Bureaus, 1978.

Koontz, Harold. *The Board of Directors and Effective Management.* New York: McGraw-Hill, 1967.

Kuenzli, Gary. *Successful Board Leadership.* Management Resource Center, YMCAs of Southern California, 1984.

Kurtz, Daniel L. *Board Liability.* Moyer Bell Limited, 1988.

Lindeman, Edward. *The Community: An Introduction to the Study of Community Leadership and Organization.* New York: Association Press, 1961.

Lippincott, Earle, and Elling Aannestad. "How Can Businessmen Evaluate the Management of Voluntary Welfare Agencies?" *Harvard Business Review* 42, no. 6 (November–December 1964): 870.

———. "Management of Voluntary Welfare Agencies." *Harvard Business Review* 46, no. 6 (1964).

Middleton, Melissa. "Nonprofit Boards of Directors: Beyond the Governance

Function." In *The Nonprofit Sector*, edited by Walter W. Powell. New Haven: Yale University Press, 1987.

Mirvis, Phillip, and Edward Hackett. "Work and Workforce Characteristics in the Non-profit Sector." *Monthly Labor Review* (April 1983).

Morgan, Mark. "Does Your Board Include Bankers? Here's How to Find Local Leaders." *Perspective Magazine*, May 1989.

Munson, Mary K. *Creative Recognition Ideas*. University of Illinois 4-H Youth, 1987.

———. *Educational Methods and Techniques*. University of Illinois 4-H Youth, 1987.

Nason, John W. *Presidential Assessment*. Washington, D.C.: Association of Governing Boards of Universities and Colleges, 1984.

———. *An Inquiry into Current Program Toward Strengthening the Performance of Board Members of Nonprofit Organizations*. Washington, D.C.: Association of Governing Boards of Universities and Colleges, 1984.

———. "Trustee Responsibilities." In *The Nature of Trusteeship*. Washington, D.C.: Association of Governing Boards of Universities and Colleges, 1982.

Naylor, Harriet H. *Volunteers Today*. Dryden, N.Y.: Dryden Associates, 1973.

Newby, Jack M., Jr. "How to Measure Your Board the Quantitative Way." *Perspective Magazine*, September 1978.

Nielson, Waldemar A. *The Endangered Sector*. New York: Columbia University Press, 1979.

O'Connell, Brian. *America's Voluntary Spirit*. New York: The Foundation Center, 1983.

———. *The Board Members Book*. New York: The Foundation Center, 1985.

———. *Effective Leadership in Voluntary Organizations*. New York: Walker and Company, 1981.

———. *Nonprofit Management Series* (9 booklets). Washington, D.C.: Independent Sector, 1988.

Olenick, Arnold J. *Making the Non-profit Organization Work: A Financial, Legal, and Tax Guide for Administrators*. Englewood Cliffs, N.J.: Institute for Business Planning, 1983.

———. *A Nonprofit Organization Operating Manual: Planning for Survival and Growth*. New York: Foundation Center, 1991.

Patton, Arch, and John C. Baker. "Why Won't Directors Rock the Boat?" *Harvard Business Review*. (November–December 1987).

Public Management Institute. *How to Be an Effective Board Member*. San Francisco: Public Management Institute, 1980.

Reno, Kyle. *Manual for Board Members of Not-For-Profit Organizations.* Denver: Technical Assistance Center, 1986.

Rudney, Gabriel. "The Scope and Dimensions of Nonprofit Activity." In *The Nonprofit Sector,* edited by Walter W. Powell. New Haven: Yale University Press, 1987.

Savage, Thomas J. *The Cheswick Process: Seven Steps to a More Effective Board.* Boston: The Cheswick Center, 1982.

Schindler-Rainman, Eva, and Ronald Lippitt. *The Volunteer Community: Creative Use of Human Resources.* Fairfax, Va.: NTL/Learning Resources Corporation, 1976.

Schoderbek, Peter P. *The Board and Its Responsibilities.* United Way of America, 1983.

Selby, Cecily Cannan. "Better Performance from Nonprofits." *Harvard Business Review* 56, no. 5 (September–October 1978): 77–83.

Seymour. *Designs for Fund-raising: Principles, Patterns, Techniques.* New York: McGraw-Hill, 1966.

Smith, David Horton. "Evaluating Nonprofit Activity." In *The Nonprofit Organization Handbook,* edited by Tracy D. Connors. New York: McGraw-Hill, 1980.

Sorenson, Roy. *How To Be a Board or Committee Member.* New York: Association Press, 1962.

———. *The Art of Board Membership.* New York: Association Press, 1953.

Sprafkin, Benjamin. *How To Become a More Effective Board Member.* Social Life Series, Richmond School of Social Work, Virginia Commonwealth University (March–April, 1968).

Swanson, Andrew. *Building A Better Board.* The Taft Group, 1984.

———. *The Determinative Team: A Handbook for Board Members of Volunteer Organizations.* Providence: Exposition Press, 1978.

Trecker, Harleigh B. *Citizen Boards at Work.* New York: Association Press, 1970.

Tropman, John E. *Effective Meetings: Improving Group Decision Making.* Sage Publications, 1980.

United Way of America. *The Citizen Board in Voluntary Agencies.* Alexandria, Va.: United Way of America, 1979.

Vineyard, Sue. *Beyond Banquets, Plaques, and Pens: Creative Ways to Recognize Volunteers and Staff.* Heritage Arts, 1981.

Volunteer Urban Consulting Group, The. *The Responsibilities of a Director of a New York, New Jersey, or Connecticut Nonprofit Corporation.* The Volunteer Urban Consulting Group, 1978.

Weber, Joseph. *Managing the Board of Directors.* New York: The Greater New York Fund, 1975.

Weisbrod, Burton A. *The Nonprofit Economy.* Cambridge: Harvard University Press, 1989.

Weisman, Carol. *Secrets of Successful Boards: The Best From Nonprofit Boards, Condensed Edition.* St. Louis, Mo.: F. E. Robbins & Sons Press, 1998.

Websites of Organizations with Useful Publications

IT Resource Center	www.npo.net/itrc
Independent Sector	www.indepsec.org
Association for Research on Nonprofit Organizations and Voluntary Action	www.arnova.org
First Nonprofit Mutual Insurance Company	www.firstnonprofit.com
The Nonprofit Times	www.nptimes.com
The Chronicle of Philanthropy	www.philanthropy.com
The Grantsmanship Center	www.tgci.com
Youth Today	www.youthtoday.org
The Alliance for Nonprofit Management	www.allianceonline.org
Better Business Bureau	www.bbb.org
GuideStar	www.guidestar.org
The Tutor/Mentor Connection	www.tutormentorconnection.org
Charity Navigator	www.charitynavigator.org
Board Source	www.boardsource.org
Jossey-Bass, Publishers	www.josseybass.com
John Wiley and Sons, Publishers	www.wiley.com
Boys & Girls Clubs of America	www.bgca.org
YMCA of the USA	www.ymca.net
YWCA of the USA	www.ywca.org
Girl Scouts of America	www.girlscouts.org
United Way of America	www.national.unitedway.org

Monographs Available from The Institute for Voluntary Organizations and The Voluntary Management Press.

For availability and ordering information, please contact us at:

Address: 4800 Prince, Downers Grove, IL 60515
Phone: (630) 964–0432
Fax: (630) 964–7510
Website: www.ifvo.org
e-mail: billconrad2@attbi.com

Board of Directors Effectiveness Tools
Condensed Parliamentary Procedure (Also in Spanish)
My Perceptions of Boards—A Self Discovery Process
The Role of the Audit Committee in Voluntary Organizations
Individual Giving: How to Ask for Contributions
Effective Board & Committee Meetings
Do Your Board Committee Meetings Motivate or Turn Off
Questions to Consider before Joining a Nonprofit Board of Directors

Assessment Instruments
Internal Climate Indicators for Voluntary Organizations
Board of Directors Self-Assessment
Management Self Assessment
Performance Assessment of the Staff Chief Executive
Performance Assessment of Board Members

Management Tools
Guidelines for Benefits
A Primer on Advocacy
Risk Management for Nonprofit Organizations
Guidelines for Public Relations for Voluntary Organizations
How to Analyze and Report Annual Giving Campaign Progress
A Framework for Analyzing and Planning an Annual Giving Campaign for
    Operating Funds
A Nonprofit Leadership/Management Operational Model